The Devil Came Down to Chinatown

The True Story of the Church's Rescue of Brothel Slaves in Old Francisco

Christine Taylor

The Devil Came Down to Chinatown

DEDICATION

This book started life as a play. I remain so grateful for Patricia James who suggested that I turn it into a book, my amazing Bible study group who always has my back, Pastor Dave, and the rest of the great people of Wrightwood Community United Methodist Church.

CONTENTS

ACKNOWLEDGMENTS

Gum Moon Women's Residence: Asian Women's Resource Center exists today as a testimony to the faithfulness of God and the courage of His people.

Introduction

"A green mansion is a place of filth and shame
Of lost chastity and lost virtue...
All the more ashamed, beyond words.
I must by all means leave this troupe of flowers and rouge;
Find a nice man and follow him as his woman." (Unknown Chinese prostitute, 19th century)

Cheating the Devil in Chinatown is a true story. These events happened, these people existed. People like Wong Ah So. Wong Ah So was a 10-year-old peasant girl in China when her mother sold her to a Chinese household as an indentured servant. Upon her release Ah So returned home, hoping to find a respectable husband and have her own household. A handsome merchant named Huey Yow visited her and her parents, and told them that a wealthy Chinese immigrant in San Francisco wanted to marry Wong Ah So. As proof he offered a generous bride price, which her parents accepted. Huey Yow paid for her ship passage and the girl boarded the freighter for the United States.

But Wong Ah So had been lied to. Instead of a husband, a new Chinese mistress with cold eyes met her at the dock and forced her into a carriage. Sing Yow told the girl that if she did not "make a fuss" she would pay off her passage in two years – by working at Sing Yow's Chinatown brothel. Paying off the ship passage would cost $1000; an incredible sum in those days. The girl was forced to go to work as a prostitute. Most of her money was taken by her mistress.

After just a year Sing Yow sold her to a different owner in Fresno, California. Her price was $2,500 in 19th century cash; about the cost of a mid-market car today. While Wang Ah So was working as a prostitute she sent a letter to her mother. Reverence for parents was fundamental to Chinese society but Ah So's suspicion that her mother knew her fate keeps breaking out in the plaintive letter.

Wong Ah So's story ended better than it began. One of her assignments was to be present as an available prostitute at a Tong banquet. To her dismay she spotted a friend of her father's there. She rejected his attempt to greet her, claiming that he had her confused with someone else.

But the friend knew about the Presbyterian Home in San Francisco and contacted the well-known rescue missionary Donaldina Cameron for help. Donaldina and her partners made the trip to Fresno, where ten days after the banquet they rescued Ah So from her owner and brought her back to safety at the Home for rescued Chinese prostitutes in San Francisco.

There Ah So learned to read Chinese and to speak English. A year after her escape she married a Chinese merchant from Boise, Idaho. In the following decades she raised a family of five daughters and three sons. She even managed to return to China where she discovered that her mother had died and left four younger siblings. Wong Ah So brought her brothers and sisters with her to the United States, and in 1835 she testified for the prosecution in the last trial involving a Chinese prostitution ring ever to be held in San Francisco.

Part 1: The Devil in Chinatown

Falling on the Gold Mountain

March 1848. "Gold! Gold! Gold from the American River!" shouted Samuel Brannan as he marched through the narrow streets of San Francisco holding up a vial of gold like a tiny torch.

How did Wong Ah So and many thousands of girls like her ended up in the United States as virtual slaves? The story starts with gold.

Samuel Brannan was bigger than life. He grew up in the East and made a name for himself living as a printer, publisher and store owner. In 1842 he heard several sermons by Joseph Smith and converted to the Church of Latter Day Saints, better known as Mormonism. He moved to New York City and began publishing newspapers for Mormon readers. He was not necessarily an obedient Mormon – when angry elders insisted he pay his tithe, he retorted that he'd give the Lord his tithe when the Lord signed the receipt. But he tired of community persecution, so with 200 others of the faithful he chartered a boat to San Francisco. They landed in 1846.

Brannan started another newspaper and founded a general store in San Francisco. The store did well in the fast-growing town, so he added a second store in Coloma, another growing town near an agricultural settlement founded by John Sutter.

Brannan was working in the Coloma store in February

1848 when construction workers from Sutter's Mill came into the store to buy supplies. Brannan collected the items and laid them out on the counter. But instead of dingy coins or dirty paper bills the men slapped down gold nuggets. Brannan snatched up the gold, pushed the goods into the men's dirty hands, and went at top speed to the construction site at Sutter's Mill where he saw excited workers picking up gold off the ground.

John Sutter met him there. He pleaded with Brannan to keep the news quiet. Sutter's dream was to build an agricultural empire in fertile California, and gold mining on his land would ruin him. He was right, it did. The floodgates were open and there was no turning back the river of gold.

Brannan immediately returned to San Francisco to outfit his local shop with miner's gear and prospecting tools. Once he was ready to sell equipment to an avalanche of prospectors, he went to his office where he printed his newspaper *The California Star*. He could not get the paper out on time – news was spreading, and his entire staff had packed up and left for the gold fields. Never one to miss an opportunity, he picked up a vial of gold nuggets he had collected at Sutter's Mill and made his famous parade through the city. "Gold! Gold on the American River!"

The California Gold Rush had begun.

Go for the Gold

The locals came first. They rushed onto the gold fields and the very early ones did pick up nuggets from the ground.

Incoming miners from all over California streamed in right after them. They did not find it quite as easy as picking it off the ground, but made fortunes with shallow, easy-to-work mines and panning. Prospectors from Oregon came next and the other western states and territories soon followed.

News traveled fast. The *New York Herald* published the story of California gold in August 1848, and President James Polk spoke before Congress to confirm the miraculous story. The United States counted its lucky stars: Mexico had ceded California as a territory to the U.S. a scant two weeks before the gold find at Sutter's Mill.

Men and a few women from all over the U.S. made the long trip to the gold country. Some of them braved overland trips through dangerous territory, and others took the longer but less dangerous sea route south around Cape Horn.

Charles Meyer wrote to his Aunt Crea describing the changes. In a letter dated February 28th, 1853 he wrote:

> "Tomorrow is the anniversary of my departure from Boston in the good ship Saml Appleton bound for San Francisco. It seems to me but a dream, I can hardly realize that I was cooped up on board a ship one hundred and forty days, and that I ever went around Cape Horn but so it is and when I come to think it over I find I have been through strange scenes in the short space of one year."

The early arrivals – the original Forty-Niners -- had already plucked the nuggets from the ground, so new prospectors learned how to pan gold from streams. Eventually enterprising souls developed simple mining technologies that allowed individuals and small groups to liberate gold ore that lay close to the earth's surface.

International prospectors soon joined the Americans and Mexicans, pouring in from Latin America, Australia, Europe, and China. Over the next 6 years, 300,000 gold-seekers would arrive seeking their fortunes in California.

The Chinese are Coming

The Chinese made up one of the largest groups of immigrants that would cause a massive shift in the urban populations of the West Coast. News of the Gold Rush first reached China in 1848. Many thousands of peasants from the province of Canton were suffering from a terrible series of civil wars, natural catastrophes, and famine when news arrived of the riches of faraway *Gum Saan* – the Gold Mountain in fabled California. Their response was overwhelming.

It was no accident that the news spread so quickly. The shipping industry that ran between Asia and American coasts saw a huge profit in thousands of Chinese boarding their ships and paying passage to the United States. Ship captains in Chinese ports distributed posters, pamphlets and maps all witnessing to the riches of California's rivers and rocks. Many Chinese answered the call, with more than 20,000 of them landing at the Port of San Francisco by 1853 alone.

The brig *Eagle* flying under the American flag was the first ship to bring Chinese to California. It was not a pleasant experience, even for peasants who were used to hunger and cold. The ship captains remanded Chinese passengers to the hold where there was little food, mostly rice. Water was scarce. In good weather they were allowed on deck if they stayed out of the sailors' way but in storms they were locked in darkness in the hold. Many of them never made it alive to San Francisco. But the gold seekers who did make it changed the face of the city and the state.

William Perkins was another first-hand observer during the California Gold Rush. He was a passenger aboard the steamer *New World* where he saw the Chinese immigrants coming to mine the Gold Mountain.

"Two hundred arrivals from the Celestial Empire were on their way to the Northern gold diggings. They were mostly dressed in the national costume, petticoat trousers reaching to the knees, big jackets lined with sheep or dog-skin, and quilted, and huge basket hats made of split bamboo. The lower part of their legs encased in blue cotton stockings, made of cloth and not knit, and is attached to shoes also made of thick cotton cloth, and with soles fully an inch in depth."

The Gold Rush Stops Rushing

But miner fortunes were hit or miss, and the merchants serving the miners were more likely to make money than their customers did. Not every merchant thrived. Many of them set up shop in roaring mining camps only to watch the camp die out within a few months, or they lost their merchandise in wildfires. Still, some of them made fortunes. Our friend the enterprising Brannan did, until he drank away his fortune and ended up an anonymous drunk in San Diego. A jeans maker named Levi Strauss founded a dynasty that lasts to this day.

Many businesses catering to the miners did not make their owners rich but made them a decent living. The Americans founded general merchandise stores, the Chinese ran laundries, and respectable women offered sewing services and respectable boarding houses.

Meanwhile the sleepy little town of Yerba Linda with a population of 200 had grown into San Francisco's 36,000 people in just 8 years. Even as the Gold Rush was grinding to halt, gold still flowed through San Francisco in the hands of big mining companies and wealthy merchants. The Golden State was officially born in 1850.

But there was another side to the romance of the Gold Rush and the city by the sea. Since the coming of the miners, some women had prostituted themselves. Every mining camp had its gaming house or saloon where lonely miners went. The prostitutes in the mining camps belonged to every race, but many of the owners favored the immigrant Chinese women for their cultural submission to authority. They favored them even more in the growing coastal cities, especially the bustling port city of San Francisco and its shadowy brothels.

Life in San Francisco's Chinatown

"The streets of Chinatown fairly swarm with its silent-footed inhabitants. They do not come and go, they appear and disappear. From dark door-ways and alleys, and from the gloomy interior of shops, these pallid-faced figures with shaven heads and dangling cues clothed in voluminous black or blue blouses and short straight trousers, their ankles swathed in white linen and their feet mounted on padded slippers, they pass and repass in spectral procession." (Robert Fletcher, Ten Drawings in Chinatown)

In the height of summer 1846 an enthusiastic gang of American miners raised the Stars and Stripes above what would be San Francisco's Portsmouth Square. Within a year, the once-small coastal town filled with people and buildings. Portsmouth Square, although it was very near the growing city center, did not fare as well. The Square remained a cleared area and served admirably as a cow pen for some time while largely Chinese businesses grew up around it. The businesses catered to miners of all nationalities: the cheap hotels and shops suited the miners' thin pocketbooks, while the gambling dens -- and worse -- suited their entertainment needs.

As the population of San Francisco grew, the Chinese-owned businesses flared out around the square until they were bounded by Dupont and Kearny Streets. People called it Little Canton, reflecting most refugees from the hard-hit province; by

1853 the press called it Little Chinatown. In 1898 writer Robert Fletcher co-published a book with artist Ernest Peixotto. They called it *Ten Drawings in Chinatown*. Fletcher wrote:

> "Chinatown was only twelve blocks in size. It held hundreds of street merchants, dozens of retail stores and herbalists, five Chinese restaurants, numerous small homes and boarding houses, modest business buildings, and the headquarters of benevolent and family associations. The Chinese laundries were the biggest business of all and the only ones to spread widely throughout the entire city -- over 7000 of them by the year 1880. By 1853 these crowded twelve blocks housed 25,000 people."

This high concentration was not exactly welcome news. In 1853 San Francisco newspaper *Alta California* pointed out that 25,000 Chinese immigrants were concentrated in a dense area bordered by a few blocks, and that they had driven out everything and everyone else. The article warned that the Chinese "are not our people and never will be, though they remain here forever... They do not mix with our people and it is undesirable that they should, for nothing but degradation can result to us from the contact... It is of no advantage to us to have them here. They can never become like us."

Not everyone felt the same way and there were positive forces in Chinatown. Immigrants from Chinese regions would band together to serve as benevolent associations to help for incoming immigrants of that same region. Large extended families would do the same. The sixth largest of them joined together in the Chinese Consolidated Benevolent Association, or the Chinese Six Companies.

The leaders of the Six Companies were high-status, wealthy Chinese who were active in San Francisco and even state politics. Given the extreme state of Chinese prejudice in the U.S. even the Six Companies could not directly speak to the political process. Instead they spoke through their highly paid and influential white American lawyers. Within Chinatown they held a virtual monopoly on political power. Many of them invested in legitimate stores and businesses like clothing and cigar factories, rice, tea and silk imports, the ever-present laundries, general stores, two theatres, and three newspapers.

Chinatown Below

Journalist Will Irwin wrote of Chinatown, "They had burrowed to a depth of a story or two under the ground, and through this ran passages in which the Chinese transacted their dark and devious affairs--as the smuggling of opium, the traffic in slave girls and the settlement of their difficulties."

In the dark streets and maze-like alleyways lived Chinatown Below: a dark world of gambling, gang wars, opium dens, and the buying and selling of human beings. Fletcher wrote about the change in the Chinatown he once knew, a dark and shadowy change.

"One can so easily imagine the respectable family that once occupied the commonplace dwelling, where the flowered wall paper was new, and there were carpets on the floor and the front parlor was the pride of the house-wife's heart, kept sacred to visitors, Sundays and funerals. Now the open hall door and grimy windows, the shameless publicity of what was once modest and retiring, is almost human in its degradation; a loss of virtue that is proclaimed by the rouge-like patches of red paper on wall and door-post, that are always the first announcement of Chinese occupancy."

Certainly, there were respectable Chinese families who lived in some of those old houses. But there was a distinct and growing criminal element that showed itself in shadowy, rundown neighborhoods.

The Problem of Prostitutes

One of the largest criminal enterprises was prostitution. By 1853 Chinatown's crowded twelve blocks housed 25,000 people -- and of these 25,000, only 10% were women. Men wanted women and they were willing to pay for them whether the women were willing or not. The brothels grew like toxic toadstools in Chinatown.

There were two types of Chinatown brothels: the parlor house and the crib. The parlor houses were expensive and exclusively served white men. This type of brothel was beautifully furnished with exotic woods, silks and embroideries, and soft beds like clouds. They smelled of perfume and opium. Their prostitutes looked healthy and were beautifully dressed – a fantasy of the compliant Chinese woman for wealthy whites. There were even a few white women serving there who were opium addicts and preferred to ply their trade close to their

Chinatown dealers.

These places were bad enough but the lower-class brothels, called cribs, were worse. Cribs were small and cheap to set up and flourished on Jackson and Washington streets and in back alleys throughout Chinatown. These places welcomed men of any race that had a few coins to spend; poor Chinese workers made up most customers.

Most of the cribs were simply one-story hovels about 12 feet wide and 14 feet deep. The interior of the small shacks was subdivided into cubicles by thick curtains. The girls lived and entertained in these four by six-foot rooms. Doors and windows were barred since the enslaved girls were not allowed to leave. Each prostitute who was not with a customer posed in her cubicle so passing men could inspect her through her barred window.

Mrs. Lee, for example, owned the biggest brothel in Chinatown with many slave girls. At 7:00 every night the girls dressed in silk and seated themselves in front of a large window that opened onto the street. Passersby would review the girls, make their choice, and go in to pay for the night.

The only way in or out was the narrow door. Customers were greeted by the crib's madam who asked him what services he required, took his money, and led him to the tiny curtained cubicle where the girl he picked was waiting.

And when the prostitutes traveled, as they might between brothels or to local Tong events, they were dressed in their distinctive attire of cheap silk pajamas. Eyes were everywhere, watching to be sure they did not run.

An American minister named Isaac Smith Kalloch was no friend to the Chinese, but his eyewitness accounts of the deplorable state of the brothels and prostitutes brings home the horror of it like no other.

"Sullivan Alley -- houses of prostitution; prostitutes soliciting there, some not over 10 or 12 years old; these latter call for a higher price -- $1.00 or $1.50, while the older ones rate at 50 cents. These women are slaves, and are sold to the proprietors of such dens at from $100 to $500. Whenever women land here from China, some Chinamen are sent to the steamer from the six Chinese Companies to claim these women as their wives, and so elude the laws. These women are then taken to Chinatown; the best looking and youngest are then turned over to the richer merchants for their personal pleasure, while the others are immediately sold to the highest bidder. The better-looking ones, after having filled the desires of said merchants, are then sold to the highest bidder, for the purposes of prostitution."

Chinese Go Home!

"The Chinese Must Go!" (Slogan of the anti-Chinese Workingmen's Party)

Many of the immigrant Chinese women were not kidnapped, but wanted to come into the country. They were following husbands or fiancés or believed that they could find a better life here. The problem was that most of them were legally barred from entering this country. The fault lay with the new Chinese Exclusion Act, which rose directly out of a tide of prejudice against the Chinese.

Chinese immigrants were first welcomed as hard and cheap labor, good for business. But as more and more of them came, white laborers felt threatened by the Chinese. They weren't the only ones. As early as 1874 white businessmen were railing against the immigrant Chinese men and their women. A real estate circular published the following invective:

"All comparisons between Irish and German immigration and that of the Chinese are unjust. The former make their homes here, buy farms and homesteads, are of the same general race, are buried here after death, and take an interest and aid in all things pertaining to the best interests of the country. The Chinese come for a season only; and, while they give their labor, they do not expend the proceeds of such labor in the country. They do not come to settle or make homes, and not one in fifty of them are married. Their women are all suffering slaves and prostitutes, for which possession murderous feuds. The public generally agreed that the Chinese laborers were hard working, perhaps more so than the Europeans or the Americans. But it is true that unlike the white or Latino groups, few of the Chinese prospectors planned to emigrate permanently to the U.S. They had come to find their fortunes so they could send money home to their families in China, eventually to return with gold and a way to climb out of horrific poverty.

A few of the early Chinese miners made modest fortunes but quickly learned that bandits often attacked and robbed Chinese who were on their way back to seaports from the gold fields. So before making the journey to the China-bound freighters, the miners melted down the gold and shaped it into common household items like pots. They rubbed black soot onto it, and then traveled unmolested to the port cities with their harmless-looking kitchen gear. Once home, they would re-melt the disguised metal into its true gold form.

As the gold got harder and harder to mine, the American miners turned actively hostile towards competing immigrant prospectors. As early as 1849 a gang of white 49ers drove off 60 Chinese men at Chinese Camp in Tuolumne County. By 1852 more white gangs had expelled Chinese miners from mining camps all over the gold fields of California. The Chinese willingness to work hard for low pay began to alarm whites; and in 1862 American miners and merchants formed an "anti-coolie" organization.

The California State Legislature came under pressure to act. They were initially reluctant to discourage Chinese labor since the laborers paid their taxes and rarely used government services. But the legislators finally bowed to voter pressure and passed a miner's tax aimed strictly at non-Americans. The tax seems low to us but to them it was astronomical -- $20 a month in the late 19th century translates to well over $500 in today's currency.

Between the machinery needed to mine the increasingly elusive gold and the mining tax, most Chinese left the mining fields by 1868. They might have returned to China, but another opportunity opened: work on the First Transcontinental Railroad. The Chinese turned their attention to working on that massive project, and a fresh wave of men came from China to join them. They also made up a huge portion of the farm workers as California developed its massive agricultural industry.

Meanwhile more Chinese massed together in the port cities of the West Coast and began offering services: restaurants, shops, and laundries -- especially laundries. An enterprising immigrant opened the first Chinese laundry in San Francisco in 1851 followed by a veritable tsunami of laundries all over the Pacific coast. The Chinese spread everywhere to work on the railroads, the farms, and cities all up and down the West Coast. And Californians looked at their exotic co-workers and neighbors and worried even more.

Protests

Earlier the U.S. had willingly drawn up the Burlingame Treaty, officially the Treaty of Tientsin, between the U.S. and China to protect Chinese immigrant rights. At the time of its signing the U.S. was eager to import Chinese immigrants because they were cheap and willing labor for the railroads and California agriculture. And since most of the Chinese immigrants sent money home to their families, China profited as well. Burlingame protected the right of the Chinese to emigrate to the U.S. and guaranteed their legal protection in this country. One clause supported "the inherent and inalienable right of man to change his home and allegiance, and the mutual advantage of the free migration and emigration of their citizens and subjects, respectively for purposes of curiosity, of trade, or as permanent residents." Another clause stated, "Chinese subjects visiting or residing in the United States, shall enjoy the same privileges, immunities, and exemptions in respect to travel or residence, as may there be enjoyed by the citizens or subjects of the most favored nation."

But public opinion was changing as the U.S. economy shifted towards higher rates of unemployment, and gold mining became less and less profitable. Franklin A. Buck spoke for many as he grudgingly admired the Chinese persistence and courage, but as immigration to the gold fields grew he displayed a worsening opinion.

Led by business owners and laborers who claimed that the Chinese were an economic threat, Western states and municipal governments passed more than 30 laws limiting Chinese rights in the face of the Burlingame treaty. The federal government followed suit in 1882 by passing the first of three draconian Exclusion Acts in 1882 that severely limited Chinese immigration into the United States.

A contemporary Los Angeles journalist, John Arroup, disapproved of the legal actions and questioned the business owners' motivations.

"I never found a strong advocate of Chinese immigration who was not actuated by fanaticism or selfishness. . . . I have seen men, American born, who certainly would, if I may use a strong expression, employ devils from hell if the devils would work for 25 cents less than a white man, even though the white man may be an American citizen who had gone through all the rebellion."

By 1871 there were four job seekers for every job in California, yet Chinese made up a disproportionate segment of laborers. They were particularly prominent in farm labor, not only because they accepted low pay (which they did) but because they were famed for their hard work ethic. This made them a convenient target for angry Californians who referred to them as "coolies" and accused them of accepting degrading slave-like positions to undermine white job seekers. In fact, Samuel Gompers, who was president of the Marxist American Federation of Labor, entitled one of his talks "Meat vs. Rice--American Manhood vs. Asiatic Coolieism. Which Shall Survive?"

Anti-Chinese immigrant groups thrived, and the press largely supported them. In 1876 *The Marin Journal* published an article on the Chinese immigrant:

> "[He] is a slave, reduced to the lowest terms of beggarly economy, and is not a fit competitor for an American freeman. That he herds in scores, in small dens, where a white man and wife could hardly breathe and has none of the wants of a civilized white man. That he has neither wife nor child, nor expects to have any. That his sister is a prostitute from instinct, from religion, education and interest, and degrading to all around her. . . . That the health, wealth, prosperity and happiness of our State demand their expulsion from our shores."

The Exclusion Acts

Public alarm at the growing number of Chinese immigrants spread to the federal Congress, which up until now had supported Burlingame. California Senator Aaron A. Sargent vilified the Chinese while speaking against the Treaty.

> "The Pacific coast must in time become either American or Mongolian. There is a vast hive from which Chinese immigrants may swarm. Upon the point of morals there is no Aryan or European race which is not far superior to the Chinese. Chinese do not come to make their home in this country, do not desire to become citizens, do not desire the ballot. The tide of Chinese immigration is gradually tending eastward and before a quarter of a century

will probably have to be met upon the banks of the Mississippi, and perhaps on the Ohio and the Hudson. The committee recommends that ... Congress legislate to restrain the great influx of Asiatics to this country."

Some people held dissenting opinions, including the chairman of Sargent's own committee. Senator Oliver P. Morton of Indiana tracked Californian economic growth to Chinese labor.

"If the Chinese in California were white people, being in all other respects what they are, I do not believe that the complaints and warfare made against them would have existed to any considerable extent. Their difference in color, dress, manners, and religion have, in my judgment, more to do with this hostility than their alleged vices or any actual injury to the white people of California."

Nevertheless, Senator Sargent's opinion carried the day. Congress voted for an Exclusion Act in the late 1870s. President Rutherford B. Hayes vetoed it, but Congress managed to overcome the veto and eventually pass it by 1882. The draconian Act completely suspended Chinese immigration for 10 years. No more Chinese were to be admitted to the country during this time, making them the only ethnic group ever to have been specifically denied entrance into America. The Act was renewed in 1892 for 10 years and again in 1902, at which time Congress did not bother to put in a terminus. As far as they were concerned the Act was permanent. (The Act remained in place until 1943, when Congress repealed it in favor of their WWII ally China.)

By 1892 the Exclusion Act had hurt missionary work in China. A report from the Methodist Episcopal Church (MEC) Missions Department in 1892 reported, "The recent anti-Chinese legislation has had an injurious effect upon our work. Many of the Chinese who were friendly toward us are now hostile to us. Questions are asked us which are not easily answered in the light of the religion we profess. It is difficult to convince a Chinaman that the Christian nation which has passed laws so hostile to his race can be sincere in its concern for his spiritual welfare. Many of our best members who had returned from a short visit to their native land have found themselves shut out by the recent Exclusion Bill. This act, passed in violation of a solemn treaty, has done much to embitter the Chinese against us and the religion we profess and teach."

Congregationalist minister D.A.L. Stone also protested the Exclusion Acts and the treatment of the Chinese immigrants.

"And now as to the treatment of those who are found on our soil. We are not left to the freedom of our own prejudices and passions. We are bound by international obligation and law. We may not transcend the stipulations into which our Government has voluntarily entered. Any infraction of these rules is not simply inhuman -- it is falsehood, treachery, bad faith, treason."

Yet the Exclusion laws passed and were passed again every 10 years like clockwork until World War II. There were already plenty of Chinese men in California, but very few women. The situation was primed for social and moral disaster.

The Poisonous Root

"My firm belief is that she is ignorant of being brought for any other purpose than that of a wife. The man has been smart enough to keep everything from her in every respect. In my own mind I am fully convinced that she has been brought for no other purpose than an immoral life. Poor child!" (Carrie G. Davis)

The system had its roots in China, where girls and young women were procured in Hong Kong or Canton and placed on ships heading to San Francisco. In Canton, desperate peasant families would commonly sell their daughters to procurers. Often the procurers would reassure the parents that they would find the girls good husbands to make the procured girls more tractable. Not every parent agreed to sell a child and in the case of a young attractive girl the procurers did not hesitate to kidnap the girls. (Kidnapping was a money-saving step on the procurers' part.) In Hong Kong many of the girls were tricked onto the boat with promises of a wealthy husband, or with the promise of a few years serving as a household servant and then freedom to marry or to earn a good living doing respectable work.

In fact, most of the teenagers and young women who came over on the freight ships never saw those promises but were sold immediately upon landing. Many of these girls were shipped to the United States in mail freighters running between

Hong Kong and Pacific coast ports in San Diego, Los Angeles, San Francisco, Portland and Seattle. One of the largest markets was in the cosmopolitan city of San Francisco where Chinese Tongs often bribed or partnered with customs agents to intercept the girl on the dock. They were quickly sold to homes as indentured servants, as concubines to merchants, or as prostitutes. Most of the young women who were sold as servants and concubines would be resold to the brothels once they aged and lost their beauty from neglect and misuse.

Most of the women were procured in China, where selling poor young women was relatively common in war- and disaster-torn Canton province. In China, an official of the Ch'ing dynasty reported that many peasant families in Canton were supported solely on the wages of a daughter turned prostitute. Some professional procurers promised that they were bringing the women to California to be married. Given the general excitement over fortunes to be made in Gold Mountain, this was a more attractive message than it otherwise might have been. Yet most of these young women were sent straight to a brothel.

Some of the women decided to go as an indentured servant in a merchant's household to pay off their passage to the U.S. A Chinese immigrant named Xin Jin borrowed the cost of her passage from a procurer, only finding once she arrived in San Francisco that her indentured servanthood was to be spent in a brothel for four and a half years… if she lived that long. The women and girls did not. There is a surviving contract dating from the 1860s. It reads:

"An agreement to assist a young girl named Loi

Yau. Because she became indebted to her mistress for passage, food, &c., and has nothing to pay, she makes her body over to the woman Sep Sam, to serve as a prostitute to serve as the sum of $503... Loi Yau shall serve four and a half years... When the time is out Loi Yau may be her own master, and no man shall trouble her. If she runs away before the time is out and any expense is incurred in catching, then Lai Yau must pay that expense. If she is sick fifteen days or more, she shall make up one month for every fifteen days." (Quoted by Wendy Rouse Jorae)

"An agreement to assist," indeed.

By 1870 census officials counted 3,536 Chinese women in California. 2,157 were listed as with the profession of "prostitute." Other surveys echoed these findings: by 1879, seventy-one percent of Chinese women in San Francisco were prostitutes. By the 1850s and 1860s the slave trade was in full swing. The Chinese Fighting Tongs operated a thriving business importing Chinese women for sale to the brothels, and there were open auctions on the San Francisco docks. In these days before Angel Island cracked down on smuggling, American inspectors were bribed to look the other way.

The Wife Game

Not all Chinese women in San Francisco were sex workers. Some were first wives who had already been admitted into the U.S. before the Act went into effect. Even single women could pursue professions like tailors and launderers, and some married women ran family businesses with their husbands. Others, especially the children, were indentured servants or *mui tsai*. Their parents were either dead or had sold them into domestic servitude. Chinese masters did not pay wages but were supposed to free their *mui tsai* when the girls reached 18, and to help them find a husband to support them. However, all too often the masters got greedy and instead of freeing the girls sold them into prostitution. They could get good money for the girls, especially in San Francisco. In contrast to a Chinese immigrant's yearly take of $500, a brothel owner could easily make $2500 per year *per prostitute*. They could afford to be generous on the purchase price.

But most of the Chinese women in San Francisco were prostitutes, the clear majority of them not out of choice. By the 1880s Chinese prostitution had become a dark and thriving business in San Francisco's Chinatown. In response a few officials and concerned volunteers began to rescue the girls that they could. In 1897, *Women's Work* magazine reported on a recent rescue of Chinese girls by customs inspectors.

> "As recently as March of this year six girls from fifteen to eighteen years of age were found by immigration inspectors close prisoners in an evil-smelling den in Chinatown in San Francisco. The girls were terrified when the officers broke down the barred door, for the proprietors of the place had told them that if white men found them they would kill them. They were pretty girls and the interpreter learned from them that they had been kidnapped from Hongkong and sold for large sums."

These girls were sent back home to China. They were lucky.

Hutchings' *California Magazine* published an article about the Chinese immigrants in 1857. To our modern ears the article sounds horrifying, but it was considered fair for that time and culture.

"Now, and it is to introduce you to your acquaintance Celestial John and his lady, types and shadows of the empire of China. A people that numbers in California, at this moment, over 40,000, half enough to form a respectable sized State -- a large majority of whom are doubtless from the lower orders, or castes; exhibiting a cringing, abject sense of servility, to that degree that it appears a fixed trait of character in all but a few of the more intelligent and wealthy.

"John (or they are all Johns) is probably the best abused foreigner we have among us. In the mines, where in many places they make a largely numerous class, though invariably minding their own business, and interfering with no one, except so far as their mere presence does it, use constantly and almost everywhere subject to abuse, extortion, and even robbery, and generally with very little hope of redress-- against which we unhesitatingly lift up our voice, believing that if our laws permit them to, come among us, our laws should certainly give to them protection, which now, unfortunately they do not."

Some of the wives came over anyway, searching for their husbands and fiancés who had stopped writing letters. They were few and far between and by the late 1800s there was one Chinese woman to every fourteen Chinese men in San Francisco, home of the largest concentration of Chinese immigrants. The government and its citizens hoped that without their women, the Chinese in America would simply die out.

Yet enterprising "businessmen," both American and Chinese, saw an opportunity in the harsh new laws. The result was a wave of commercial human trafficking. White men may prefer white women but there was a growing population of Chinese men in the cities of the West Coast, particularly in San Francisco. These men were merchants, laundry owners, restaurant workers, and laborers. There were so few of their native women in the U.S. and they were lonely for female companionship. So, Americans went to China and advertised for women to come to this country, promising to find them husbands. Some came on their own; some Chinese girls were sold to the smugglers. In any case, once they got on the ship and got to the port of San Francisco they became essential slaves and were sold into prostitution, domestic service, or sham marriages where their "husbands" sold them to someone when they got tired of their new wives.

The Journey to Slavery

"Two Slaves Less: If the good women of the Chinese Mission in San Francisco keep up their lick, our own Chinatown will soon be robbed of its female chattels. Last night Mrs. Green came up from the Bay and captured two more of these women who had tired of their lives of slavery. They will be taken down this morning." (The Sacramento Daily Union, February 1894)

With a huge demand for passage to California, in 1868 steamships began making the ocean journey between China, and Japan and the American cities of the West Coast. San Francisco's main provider was the Pacific Mail Steamship Company which provided four steamships sailing between San Francisco, Yokohama in Japan and Hong Kong. The ships carried mail and carried passengers.

In his records, Captain Stephen Splivalo described the conditions on board the steamer Alaska. Well-off white passengers were comfortable in ship's cabins but the Chinese poor who could only afford the lowest ticket (or whose ticket had been paid for by slave brokers) were huddled together in the hold. Partitions separated the women and children from the men. Buckets were the only sanitation and food was cooked rice with pork fat. Water was scarce and severely rationed. In fair weather they could come on deck in small groups but in storms they remained in the hold, which was dark even during the daylight hours and constantly vibrated from the ship's engines.

On Nov. 24, 1887 the *Daily Alta California* newspaper published an account of the slave trade called "The Bound Ship: Infamous Traffic: Stories Told by Two Chinese Girls Who Came on the Belgic."

"Yesterday morning Lee Moon Lum Shee the Chinese procuress was arraigned in the United States District Court. She pleaded not guilty to the charges preferred against her, and the case was continued until Monday next.

"Out of the twenty-five Chinese females brought here on the steamer Belgic five have been examined. The statements of three of the girls were published at length in the Alta of Wednesday. The statements of the other two were taken yesterday.

"Wong Chow Pong told a straightforward story from the start. She said she did not speak English and did not want to stop in San Francisco. On being cross-questioned she said: 'My right name is Kong How Yock. I am 16 years old. I never was married. My father and mother are in China. My home is at Hi Mun close to Hongkong. I do not want to land in San Francisco. I want to go back there. My mother sold me for $640! I will not tell the man's name that bought me. I do not know his name. My brother Hong Ah Sou, age 17, died, and that is the reason my mother sold me.'

"The other woman, Jung Ah Yung, testified at first as follows: 'Am a seamstress by occupation and was born in China. Resided formerly in this city on Dupont Street, near Washington, and left here November 22, 1881, on the [ship] City of Rio. First arrived in the United States November 6. 1877. Do not know who bought my return ticket to China. I was married in China in 1883, and the following year my husband, Lee Yun, returned to San Francisco. My father, Cheong Ching Yum, is now in China.' She afterward made the following confession: 'I never was in this country before and was never married. I can read and write. I do not want to land in San Francisco, as I know I would have to be a prostitute. I want to go back to China, where my parents are. My right name is Lou Don Tai.'

"The steamer Peking is due today from China. She has 165 Chinese passengers, and it is expected that a great many of those are Chinese girls brought here for immoral purposes. The Peking brings more women than any other steamer trading between this port and China. She is so much more commodious, and the upper deck is open and affords an excellent promenade for the women. The Belgic departs on Tuesday next and it is expected that upward of 1000 Chinese will leave on her."

Slave Markets

The smuggled women were taken to the unofficial slave

market close to the docks. Located on Dupont Street, the warehouse was informally known as the Queen's Room where women were brought for inspection and auction.

Officially, prostitution in the brothels was supposed to pay the cost of girl's ship transport and was to last no more than 4 years. However, most did not make it that long. Once at the brothels the women were only useful until pregnancy or disease occurred. Pregnancy earned another year of service; disease was a death sentence. There were no wages and no off-days except minimal stretches of time for their monthly periods. These girls worked for twenty-five to fifty cents per client. This was more money in the 1800s than it is today, but even then, it was a low price and these brothels were popular with the working men. If the girls lived out their years of service and were finally released, it was with no money or job skills, and most of them were ill.

John H. Wise was a customs collector and chief of the San Francisco Chinese Bureau in 1895. He wrote that he would, "Do as much as I can to discourage Chinese from sending for their alleged wives and children. I am satisfied that ... many women and young girls would be brought for immoral purposes. It is well known that the cunning of Chinese often circumvents the vigilance of the officers."

The Story of Ah Yung

A Methodist Episcopal Church (MEC) pastor named N. R. Johnston was visiting Beulah Park in Oakland when he found a young Chinese woman wandering the park and moaning in despair. He took her to the Methodist Mission where she told her story through an interpreter. Ah Yung was just twenty-two years old.

A man named Woo Yuen Chee bought and married Ah Yung, but marriage was little protection for a young Chinese woman. She bore two children in two years, but the first child died in infancy, and the second was kidnapped and sold by her husband's brothers when it was only fifteen months old. Ah Yung's husband left her and returned to China.

Her brothers-in-law were not done. They informed her that they were going to sell her again, but she resisted them. After beating her they hired highbinders to kidnap her and kill her. Fortunately, the highbinder could not bring himself to murder the young woman in cold blood. Instead he sent Ah Yung to Oakland, told her never to return to Sacramento, and reported to the brothers that he had killed her. He used the money they paid him to return to China.

Ah Yung was not alone in her story. Chinese men frequently married multiple wives and kept concubines and these women could be sold when their "husband" grew tired of them. Even if the husband kept the wife, in-laws felt no such compunction.

The Highbinders

The Chinese Gangs were hip deep in the slave trade. *The San Francisco Examiner* trumpeted, "It is time for people with the instincts of humanity to pay some attention to the proceedings in the courts with reference to the wretched Chinese women bought and sold by their masters, who speculate in their degradation."

The *Examiner* editorial went on to condemn the Chinese gangs and their foot soldiers the highbinders.

> "This work has been carried on literally at the point of the revolver against the unremitting opposition of the murderous highbinders, who have been outlawed in their own country and make assassination and every species of crime their profession in this. The odds are fearful, but one would think in such a contest as this the Mission could at least rely on the support of the laws of its own country.

> "The first resort of the highbinders, when a victim escapes to the protection of the Mission, is to the American courts. They can always find lawyers who, for a fee, are willing to aid them.

> "The highbinder is not content with making a straightforward fight. He attempts to drive from the witness stand the modest Christian women, whose lives are devoted to the work of helping these unfortunate Chinese girls, his plan being to ask them wholly unnecessary, irrelevant and in-delicate questions in the coarse language of the slums. He takes a positive delight in his unclean work, and announces his intention of keeping up his infamous war on the Mission until his work is accomplished.

"The thing must stop. The laws of California are adequate to protect a band of good women unselfishly working in the cause of humanity and decency; and the public only needs to know what is going on to make its voice heard in a way that will be respected."

Highbinder wars had a direct effect on the missions located in Chinatowns up and down the West Coast. The 1894 MEC annual domestic missions report complained about highbinder activity in Sacramento. The Rev. F. J. Masters, a leader in the Methodist Mission work, told the following story:

"On the 24th of February 1890, word was sent to the Methodist Mission that a young widow named Chun Kook was about to be sold to a slavery worse than death. Her husband, to whom she had been married but a few months, died very suddenly, and immediately after his funeral the widow, who is a very pretty little woman, was taken possession of by her husband's clan. Two big Chinamen, said to be highbinders, were guarding her. The ladies of the Mission and the superintendent undertook to rescue her. We were met by the strongest opposition on the part of the men. They grappled with us, and a hand-to-hand wrestle took place, in which the Chinese became convinced of the superiority of Anglo-Saxon muscle. The woman was rescued and safely housed in the Mission with the household effects which belonged to her. Two more amazed and disgusted looking men could not be found than these Chinamen appeared when balked of their prey."

The Madams

Some Chinese women were in partnership with the Tongs. These brothel madams ranged from little more than prostitutes themselves to wealthy slaveowners. Most of them started off as slaves themselves, who over the years saved enough money to launch themselves into the same business.

One madam earned quite a name for herself. Ah Toy was born in China. She wrote that she desired to "better her condition" so she and her husband took ship from Hon Kong in 1849 and sailed to the United States. However, her husband died on the voyage. She was a tall, beautiful woman and with cold practicality she became the mistress of the ship's captain in exchange for gold to start her new life. With her beauty, height and exotic bound feet she was a sight to see in San Francisco and she became infamous as the "girl in the green silk pantaloons." She supported herself by becoming a high-priced courtesan to several wealthy white men. With her income she bought her own prostitution business off San Francisco's Clay Street, in an alley known as Pike Street.

American entertainment sometimes glorifies the "prostitute with the heart of gold." But the only heart that Ah Toy seemed to have was made from lead. She grew her business by buying girls from China -- one of them as young as 11 years old. She put them to work in her brothel where they endured a much darker existence than Ah Toy ever did.

The business offered peep shows and services. Any man who could afford to spend an ounce of gold -- about $16 -- could come into her brothel on Waverly Place and peep at Ah Toy through a window. The placard in front of her shop listed a menu of these delights: the "two bittee lookee" up to a "four bittee feelee," and a "six bittee doee." Her prostitutes mostly carried out these services for only wealthy men could afford a few hours with the rarified Ah Toy.

She was an astute business woman. She was tremendously impressed with the American judicial system and often used it to her advantage. In a culture where both Chinese and American women found it hard to be heard, she sued cheating customers who paid her in brass filings instead of gold. She also made speeches defending the role that prostitution played in society.

Her first court appearance went mostly unnoticed but the second made an impression. She entered the court dressed in an exotic apricot satin jacket and green pants, bright bindings on her bound feet, and rice powered face that glowed beneath her black hair.

She was suing two customers for trying to pass off brass filings as gold for payment. Ah Toy explained that she had discovered the deception herself. The judge stated that he found the accusation hard to believe. So, Ah Toy pointed out others in the courtroom who were also guilty of this crime. The court erupted in laughter when Ah Toy followed up by presenting a china basin full of brass filings as evidence. The charges against the men were dropped but the press loved her.

In another court case the *Alta California* reported favorably on the madam. "San Francisco's most renowned Chinese madam planned to sue a notorious Chinese leader for extortion. The beautiful Miss Ah Toy claimed that Yee Ah Tye had demanded her Dupont Street prostitutes pay him a tax. She promptly outsmarted him by doing something she never could have done in China -- threatening to take him to court."

Ah Toy was not as popular with law enforcement who arrested her several times for "keeping a disorderly house." Eventually Ah Toy gave up her business and disappeared from San Francisco. From there her trail grows cold.

Ah Toy may have been a popular figure in San Francisco, but as national newspapers published stories of Chinese madams the public was shocked. In 1876 Congress passed the "Act to Prevent the Kidnapping and Importation of Mongolian, Chinese, and Japanese Females for Criminal and Demoralizing Purposes," so states could pursue the local madams. The *Daily Alta California* commented in an article dated July 8, 1876.

"A case testing the ability of the authorities to convict Chinese women who hold, under an Illegal contract, Chinese girls for immoral purposes, was on bearing before United States Commissioner Sawyer, yesterday. The defendants are Shin How, alias Ah Foo, the proprietor of a Chinese house of prostitution, and Ah Shin, a procuress.

"About ten months ago she brought a Chinese

girl, seventeen years of age, from her parents in China, having given the girl's father $186 for her. The girl voluntarily entered into a contract to serve as a prostitute for a term of five years, in consideration of the sum paid her father, and in liquidation of her passage money to San Francisco. Both defendants, on several occasions, acknowledged it to the policeman, not thinking that by so doing they were making themselves amenable to the law. By an Act of Congress, the importation of women under such contracts is illegal, and the persons making the contract are subject to imprisonment for a term not exceeding five years. The case has been taken under advisement."

The Devil Came Down to Chinatown

Madam Suey Hen

"Two baby girls had been left exposed -- that is, to die, you know. They were born after me and my father said often, 'She is too many.'" (Chinese madam Suey Hen)

Not all madams were unrepentant. Infamous madam and slaveowner Suey Hin accepted Christ and tried to do the right thing by her girls. On April 2, 1899 a story from Helen Grey ran in the Sunday Edition of *The Call*. Entitled "Suey Hin: Confessions," it was subtitled "How She Bought Her Girls, Smuggled Them into San Francisco, & Why She Has Just Freed them."

When Suey Hin was a five-year-old in China her father sold her into slavery. She was brought to the United States and eventually gained her freedom, only to become a madam and slaveowner herself. She kidnapped or bought seven girls from China at the then-astronomical cost of $8300 and pressed them into service in San Francisco.

She seemed to be the natural enemy of Christian women in this country. But instead of hating her, they set out to convert her. She had no intention of becoming a Christian; she believed nothing that the "white teachers" said about Jesus. But she did understand that these women, especially the "lassies" of the Salvation Army, could be helpful to her if her girls got sick or were kidnapped by the highbinders, ~~or got sick.~~ The Salvation Army had influence with clinics and hospitals, and frequently worked with the San Francisco police to bring down violent highbinders.

Suey Hin decided to build a friendship with the Salvation Army women for those reasons. She thought she was being shrewd when she invited the women to come to her rooms and pray with her. They quickly agreed. They accompanied her to her crowded sitting-room with its great carved and canopied bed, its shrine and burning incense sticks. Prayers to the money gods were punched into scarlet paper and hung on the altar. Confronted with the pagan altar, the Salvation Army women might have beat a hasty retreat -- but they did not. They knelt with Suey Hen and two of her seven slave girls and prayed.

Suey Hen and the girls did not speak English. She did not understand the women's prayers and felt that her ruse was going well. What she did not know is that the women's prayer launched an offensive against the demonic forces right in that room.

The ladies finished their prayers and left. Suey Hen thought no more about the prayers the rest of that day. But that night, for the first time in years, she remembered her beautiful old home in Shantung and the innocent child she had been. She remembered how life was before she was forced into the life, and later how she began to buy and sell young girls.

Over the next several months Suey Hin invited the ladies back several times. Each time the women prayed intently and each time Suey Hin questioned her lifestyle even more.

She was slowly learning English, and began to think about the Jesus that the Salvation Army ladies loved. She knew that He did not approve of slave ownership. But she had a lot of money invested in her slave girls. Ah Lung and Ah San would sell for $1300. Hom Get, Man Yet and Who Sing would bring $1200 apiece. Ah Ho and Ah Ching were sick, but still worth $1000 on the market. And little Ah San was only 3 years old, but she was worth at least $300. On top of that she would also have to pay off her Tong partners. She would lose over $10,000 dollars in total were she to free her slaves – a huge amount of money in those days. On the other hand, Jesus asked "What good does it do to gain the whole world if you lose your own soul?" (Mt. 16:26)

Suey Hin struggled with the question for months. Finally, she left the girls in charge of a woman she trusted and went on retreat. For weeks she lived in a small room and thought and prayed. After several weeks she reached a conclusion. Gaining the world and its gold was not worth her eternal soul. She would accept Christ and free her slaves. One day she told her story to the writer who recorded it in Suey Hin's broken English:

"I am old, very old, too old to be an American. I like Americans, and if I were younger I would be one. Long, long ago I was born in Shantung, where the flowers are more beautiful and the birds sing more sweetly than in any other place. But my people were poor. There was not enough for all our stomachs. Two baby girls had been left exposed-- that is, to die, you know. They were born after me and my father said often, 'She is too many.'

"Once there was an old woman came to our house and she looked at me. I was 5 that year, 6 the next. When she looked at me I was afraid and I hid myself behind my mother. My father told the old woman to go away. But that night she came back again and talked to my father and mother. She put a piece of gold money in my hand and told me to give it to my father. I did, for I wanted nothing to do with her. I had enough; yes, I had plenty to eat! But that night the old woman carried me away, and I kicked and screamed and said I would not go. I do not remember much more about the beginning. I remember the ship, and I remember playing with other little girls. We were brought to San Francisco, and there were five or ten of us and we all lived with a woman on Ross alley. Every little while someone would come and see us, and as we grew older the girls were sold.

"One day it was my turn. They said I was 14 years old, but I was really 12. I don't know how much I cost, but I know both my hands were filled three times with all the gold they would hold. They money, you know, is always put in a girl's hand when she is sold. Well, then I was a slave for ten years. There was a man who loved me, but he was a poor washman, and he worked eight years and saved all, all the time. I saved all I could get, too, but it took eight years before we had saved $3000. Then we bought me from my owner and we were married."

Suey Hin hoped for a happy ending to her story but that was not to be. Three years later her husband got sick and died. She spent the little she had on a little house and a ticket to China.

"Then pretty soon I went back to China, but I did not go to my own village. No, my parents would not want to see me. I went to Hongkong and I bought three girls. Two of them are dead, but Ah Moy, she was a baby, and I paid her father 50 cents for her. After I had returned here a few months I went back to China again. I wanted to see my village, always I wanted to go back to my home. So I went, but I didn't let anybody know I was there. I went to the place where they put the babies to die. There was a baby there."

In Canton province, peasant parents depended on sons and disregarded daughters. Many baby girls were summarily placed in a small manger in the center of villages, where someone would pluck them out to raise or sell, or the infant was left to die.

"A little bit of a brown baby, and she didn't look much good anyway. But I wanted someone from my own village, and so I took the baby, and she is Ah Lung. Don't you think she is a pretty girl now? She's not a slave you know. She's a good girl, much the same as white girls. She comes from

Shantung, so I say she shall never be like the others. Slave girls most all die soon. It's bad, yes, and only the girls who want to be good and the dear Jesus knows about that. You see she is a girl and her people sold her, so what can she do?

During that trip she bought four more girls and brought them back to the United States. She put all the girls except Ah Lung into a brothel. She went back one more time and brought back six of them. To keep them from telling the truth to the American inspectors, she coached them to say they were going to be married to respectable husbands. She also warned them not to let the white men take them.

"I told the girls if they made any mistakes the white devils would get them. I said white men liked to eat China girls, they like to boil them and then hang them up to dry and then eat them. Oh, the girls didn't make any mistakes when the inspector asked them questions and when they were landed they didn't want to run away. I told them that the girls only stayed at the missions till they got very fat and then Miss Cameron and Miss Lake sold them. Oh, I was bad--wasn't I bad? But I love Jesus now."

She outright sold one girl to another madam but kept the others. After she came to believe in Christ, she freed them.

"All the other girls are here now. I will not make them bad any more. They are all free--they may go or they may stay, but I watch where they go. Hom Get, she is going to China. I bought her in

Hongkong. You want to talk to her?"

She did. Hom Get talked through an interpreter.

"Oh yes indeed, I'm going home. I'm going back to my own home. My father didn't sell me; he would not do it. He just wrote a letter to me. You want to see it? My father he loves me and he doesn't forget. I was stolen. You see my father he quarreled with a man. The man wanted to do him harm. So this wicked man he got another man who knew my father and who lived in Hongkong to write me to visit his family. My father didn't know his enemy was doing anything and he let me go. Then the man took me down town and lost me so my father's enemy could find me. Then my father's enemy sold me to Suey Hin and she brought me here.

"My father did not know where I was till the white teachers wrote to him in China. The teachers said I was freed because Suey Hin loved Jesus. Then my father wrote this letter and he sent $70. Isn't that such a lot of money? Don't you think my father loves me? And I'm going home and I will see my sister and I'll see my two brothers, but I, oh, I don't know, you see I'm not like all the other girls at home now. I love Jesus, yes, but then--. You want to see the letter my father wrote?"

Just then the girls Man Get, Ah Ho and Ah Chung came into the room. They greeted Suey Hin and shook hands with the writer. Ah Ching gave a piece of blue ribbon and a pair of long blue silk stockings to Man Get who looked sad as she took the blue things and patted them gently. Man Get had just found out that her father had died, and before he died he had tried to sell her back into slavery. Suey Hin explained.

"She has just heard her father is dead. I bought her in Victoria. When I wanted to love Jesus I thought I would ask her father to take her home and get her married. I wrote to him, but he is a very bad man. He went right to a man, showed my letter and said: 'You are going to San Francisco. That fool woman gone crazy. You buy Man Get. I sell her cheap.'"

The buyer, a man named Loo Chee, bought the girl sight unseen from her father and traveled to San Francisco to take Man Get back with him. When he met with Suey Hin he lied about the sale. He told her that he was there as a favor to Man Get's father, that he would take her safely home where she would be married. She believed him but before he went to buy train tickets he dropped a piece of paper on the floor. Ah San saw it and brought it to Suey Hin who saw that it was a bill of sale. They showed the paper to the writer.

"BILL OF SALE

Loo Wing to Loo Chee--

April 16--Rice, 6 mats, at $2.

April 18--Shrimps, 50 lbs., at $12.

April 20--Girl, $250."

Suey Hin refused to let Loo Chee back in the door. The man immediately went to the Kwai Kung Tong to complain that the former madam was keeping his legal property from him. Fong San, a representative of the Tong, came to see Suey Hin.

While Suey Hin was talking a toddler came into the room and laid a doll on Helen's lap. The child was dressed like a boy.

"Lung gave me" the child said to Helen, the writer.

"You are a boy and like dolls?"

"I not boy, I girl; I Ah San."

Helen looked at Suey Hin, who explained "Oh yes, she's a girl. I dress her like a boy so the mission people will not steal her. I very cute! They see I bring her up for a slave girl and then they come and rescue her. Oh, no, no, not at all! I make her look like a boy."

"Where did you get her?"

"Bought her. Bought her when she was ten days old. She's smart. Ah San, come here. Oh, she understands everything! Now, Ah San, sing 'Jesus Loves Me.'" The little one repeated the song then recited Psalm 23, all in very good English.

"What will you do with her?" Helen asked.

Suey's face fell. "I don't know; maybe give her to the mission. Do you want to go to the mission, Ah San?" The little girl's face clouded and she began to cry. Suey gathered her up in her arms as the child cried "I good, I good girl, Suey."

Suey Hin's and Helen's eyes were wet with tears. "What will you do with the other girls?" Helen asked.

"Oh, I suppose they get married. Only they must marry Christians. I Christian now, and I work always now for Jesus. I used to work hard for the devil, him you call Satan, but now I work harder for Jesus."

Part 2: God with Us -- The Church Militant

The Devil Came Down to Chinatown

The Church Reacts

"While the gospel is the same and also the general capacity of the people, whether they be Chinese, Japanese, or Indians, their capacity for the gospel is likewise the same. There is the same human nature, the same need, the same power to comprehend the gospel, and the gospel has the same power of producing conviction of sin, confession, repentance and receiving the pardon of sin and the regeneration, the cleansing and the filling of the Holy Spirit." (World-wide Evangelization: The Urgent Business of the Church)

Christian missionaries traveled to China as early as the 8th century. It caught on so quickly that a 9th century emperor decreed that Christianity was illegal. The Chinese church resurged under Mongol rule up until the Ming dynasty. In the 16th century the Jesuits established a new foothold by introducing Western astronomy, science and mathematics. More missionaries entered China in the 17th and 18th centuries. Then with the coming of missionary Robert Morrison, modern missionary efforts that concentrated on writing and speaking native languages began in earnest. Morrison translated a Chinese version of the Bible and an English-to-Chinese dictionary.

1814 saw another generation of hostile emperors who expelled non-Chinese missionaries and persecuted native believers. The contemporary *Missionary Herald, Volume 17* commented, "The polytheism of ancient China—the worship of hills, rivers, deceased men and women, &c; the worship of living human beings; Buddhism, Shamanism, and Lamanism, as well as atheism, are all tolerated in China. The Monotheism of the Arabian Prophet [Islam], is also tolerated; why then their hatred to the name of Jesus!"

Missionaries believed that they should be "hearers of the word and not doers only" (James 1:22) and so established schools and clinics in addition to preaching the Word. Most of the missionaries were men as were the Chinese converts, but they did not ignore women's missions. Missionaries worked with the merchant and upper classes to abolish the foot binding practices that horrified them, and to convince them to treat their indentured maids more kindly. They also distributed food to the poor, opposed the horrific opium trade, and founded mission schools that taught poor boys *and* girls at no charge to destitute families.

In the mid-19th century missions lost ground in the interior of China due to civil wars, protests against foreigners, bandits, and famine. In the 1860s when the Gold Rush started, the Protestant missions had dwindled to five coastal Chinese cities. (By the end of the 19th century everything would change with the great mission revival under J. Hudson Taylor and the China Inland Mission.)

The Chinese and the Church in America

American churches gave generously to the foreign Chinese missionary work but reacted differently to the rush of Chinese immigrants to the United States. Still, a few churches took these words from the Bible seriously: "Love the sojourner, therefore, for you were sojourners in the land of Egypt" (Deut. 10:19) and "Here there is not Greek and Jew, circumcised and uncircumcised, barbarian, Scythian, slave, free; but Christ is all, and in all." (Col. 3:11).

Several denominations banded together to help the Chinese immigrants. The Oriental Workers Association rose from the combined efforts of the Baptists, Disciples, Congregationalists, Friends, Episcopalians, MEC and Presbyterians. Two denominations founded ministries in Chinatown that were dedicated to rescuing Chinese prostitutes and children: the Methodist Episcopalians and the Presbyterians.

Not that these denominations were bastions of cultural freedom. They were children of their time, firmly believing that the Chinese immigrants should adopt American ways and abandon their "barbarian" culture. Nevertheless, they were serious about bringing Christ into Chinatown, and many of them would risk their fortunes, health and lives to do so.

Understandably, Chinese Christians opposed American's deep-seated prejudice against the Chinese. California's Governor John Bigler frequently made racist remarks against the Chinese and passed several harsh laws that unfairly taxed Chinese immigrants. Chinese Christians Norman Asing (Yuan Sheng), and Tong Achick (Tang Maozhi), protested the Governor's actions. The United States Supreme Court, hardly a friend to the Chinese, later struck down most of Bigler's laws as unconstitutional.

The Story of Jee Gam

The Chinese were not silent. The Chinese press and churches inveighed against the Exclusion Act from the beginning. In 1892 Congress extended the Exclusion Act another 10 years. Chinese immigrant and Congregationalist minister Jee Gam vigorously protested in his essay "Chinese Exclusion, from the Standpoint of a Christian Chinese" in the *American Missionary*.

At 14 years old, Jee traveled with his gold miner uncle to the United States. He found work as a servant for the Rev. George and Sarah Mooar who converted Jee to Christianity. In 1895 he was ordained as the first Chinese American Congregationalist minister, although ironically, he was not allowed to become an American citizen.

He wrote "I am a Chinaman and a Christian. I am not any less Chinese for being a follower of Christ. My love to Jesus has intensified rather than belittled my love for my native country. I am proud of China, for it is a great country. I admire her, for she has a wonderful future. What a glorious nation she will be when she embraces Christianity! I praise her authentic history, for it goes back 4,800 years.

"I honor all things that are honorable in my country. I blush for whatever has marred her record. I pray for her daily, that she may speedily become a Christian nation.

"I am in some sense also an American, for I have lived in America almost twice as long as in China. I love this country. I teach my children who are Native-born Americans to sing the National anthems. And just as I rejoice for whatever is honorable to America, and commend her example to my countrymen, so I am pained when unjust and oppressive laws are permitted to be placed upon her statute books. Such a law as the Geary Act seems to me to be one that dishonors America, as well as injures my countrymen and my native land."

In the article Jee tackled accusations against the immigrant Chinese including the fact that they imported their food (they paid heavy taxes on imported rice), did not assimilate (they were not allowed to) they did not dress in Western styles (why should Oriental dress invite persecution) and they cheapened labor wages (it wasn't the Chinese; it was the poor laborers from Europe). As to the accusation that the presence of the Chinese lowered American morals, Jee pointedly asked if American morality was so weak as to be threatened.

As a pastor he also wrote about Christian responses to evangelizing the Chinese. Far too many clergy and churches were prejudiced against the Chinese and did not want to bring them to Christ. This he found hard to accept, and pointed out that most of Chinese converts to Christianity in this country eventually went home to China, where they were instrumental in witnessing to their family and communities. "It is unchristian," Jee wrote, "for it is contrary to the teaching of Christ."

The Story of Chan Hon Fan

A Chinese immigrant named Chan Hon Fan was born in China, and his parents immigrated to San Francisco when he was a small child. As a boy he accepted Christ through the

MEC Mission in San Francisco. By the time Fan was 10 years old he was known as the "boy street preacher." He never stopped preaching. Over the next 25 years he became an ordained deacon in the MEC and moved from San Francisco to pastor to Chinese congregations in Tacoma, Washington and Portland, Oregon.

He also made the time to protest irresponsible writings from white pastors who protested the presence of Chinese in the U.S. In 1886 he wrote a Letter to the Editor in response to a published diatribe by one Rev. E. Trumbull Lee. *The Oregonian* ran the letter in its entirety and entitled it "A Chinaman's Letter." The editor wrote an introduction to the letter insisting that the letter used the exact words of Chan Hon Fan. They made no changes in printing it. The editor then wrote, "As an appeal to an insensate rabble it will be wasted, of course; for even the marvelous words of Jesus of Nazareth only impelled men to crucify him; but it ought at least to lead Rev. E. Trumbull Lee back to the words of the Master, and send him to his closet and to his knees." Mr. Fan wrote:

> "Having read over and over carefully the article of Mr. Lee I am convinced that the sentiment of it is not only 'calculated to make riot and bloodshed' but it also misrepresents a class of respectable law-abiding citizens of this fair city…. But at such a time as this, when the Chinese are everywhere exposed to danger and annoyance, both of property and in life, what benefit can it be for Rev. E. Trumbull Lee to write such false things about the Chinese? This is too mysterious even for those whom he termed the

'almond-eyed, unclean and immoral, pagan Chinese' to comprehend. A man like him brags about 'our better civilization' and glorious religion that the Chinese cannot compare with! Why not use his time and brain to write about what the meaning of the word civilization is and how to live to be called civilized people.... [Rev. Lee] might preach a sermon on the 'golden rule,' tell what the Savior said that, 'Therefore, all things whatsoever ye would that men do to you do ye even so to them'.... By so doing, I think the Chinese might be Christianized easier here than in their 'own lands,' because here they have a great deal more good teachings by example of good Christian people.

"But if Mr. Trumbull Lee thinks... that the 'Chinese are far more likely to be made Christians in their own lands by our devoted missionaries there, than they are here in contact with the lowest orders of American society—gamblers, speculators, profane men and women, and commercial and political scoundrels of every sort,' of course any man with common sense knows that it is not the fault of the Chinese that they are surrounded by the 'lowest orders of American society;' and if such is the case how can the Chinese see the beauty and excellency of Christianity...?

"Therefore, in the name of God and humanity I entreat you, Rev. Mr. Lee, to not lower yourself by sympathizing with the lawless persons on the

Chinese question, but let the true beauty and excellency of Christianity be more seen through your good sentiments and Christ-like example and then the 'pagan Chinese' can better comprehend and better appreciate and may adopt your 'better civilization' and Christian religion, but not otherwise. Yet why should the Chinese go? For 'God hath made of one blood all nations of men for to dwell on all the face of the earth.' We are here by the invitation of the United States government, and will be protected here by the stipulation of international treaty rights, as the American citizens are protected by our government in China."

The Gibsons in China

"The Chinese truly verify the Scripture statement that in this world 'there be that are called gods many and lords many.' The whole land is full of idols, and all the people are filled with idolatrous superstitions." *(Otis Gibson)*

Otis Gibson was a Methodist Episcopal minister who was born in 1826 on a New York farm. Some people lose their faith after a tragedy, others find it; and Otis accepted Christ at the age of 13 following a brother's sudden death. He would spend the rest of his life on the mission field, seeking to bring others to Christ. At 19 he joined the MEC and attended Dickinson College. He took some time to teach and accepted a temporary post at a Society of Friends (Quaker) settlement in Maryland where he met his future wife Eliza Chamberlain.

Eliza was born Elizabeth Chamberlain in 1830 to a Quaker family living in Brazier Falls, New York. As a young girl she felt a call to a life of service to God and entered a women's seminary where she earned a teacher's certificate. She was teaching in Maryland when she met the young Methodist minister Otis Gibson. Her parents were unhappy about her choice – heaven forbid she should marry a Methodist -- but the young couple married anyway, in a Methodist camp meeting at that.

Otis graduated from Dickson and was ordained in the MEC. He and Eliza sought a posting in China and were appointed as missionaries to Foochow in Canton Province. The young couple was thrilled about going on the mission field, but they encountered delay after delay.

In October 1854 they received the telegram that they were to travel to New York for sailing on the 10th. They went but learned that the ship had received orders not to sail.

In late December they were again ordered to New York as a ship was about to sail for China. They met Dr. and Mrs. Wentworth who were going to the same mission. While the Wentworths left on the ship, the Gibsons did not – the captain did not have the couple on their manifest and left them standing on the dock. Apparently, the Recording Secretary of the M. E. Missionary Society had forgotten to record Otis's appointment to the Foochow Mission.

He would not receive another appointment until next spring in March. Meanwhile the couple was sent to New Haven to study Chinese with Dr. White, a former missionary to China. They returned home to northern New York State. They were there for a week when another telegram appeared – a ship was leaving, and they were due back in New York City immediately.

The Gibsons finally boarded the clipper R.B. Forbes. But the day they were to sail a huge storm blew up along the coast of New York and the captain delayed the voyage for a day. They spent the night on board. They headed into the city early the next morning to have breakfast and barely returned on time – the ship was about to leave without them. They ran up the gang plank, the sailors raised anchor, and the Gibsons were finally on their way to China in April 1855. Eliza kept a detailed account of their journey.

"Our fellow-passengers were Dr. and Mrs. Fish. Mrs. Fish was a lovely girl of eighteen years, whom we learned to love. The day proved beautiful. The sun shone. There was a gentle breeze, and we congratulated ourselves that probably we should not be seasick. The day was enjoyed and the next until about 4 p. m., when the wind began to rise. The ship rolled and pitched some, and we quietly, one by one, turned pale and went to our state rooms. We were seen no more on deck for days. I will draw a veil right here but must tell one incident.

"The second night as we were supposed to be asleep, I heard an order given to pump ship. Now I know nothing of ship ways, but had read of pumping ship when filling with water and danger of sinking. Mr. Gibson was asleep in the upper berth and I would not waken him as I only wished that, like him, I could go down without knowing of our peril. The ship would rise on a wave and tremble and shake and settle, and I could feel it sinking. Then it would rise again and tremble and shake and sink. I kept thinking how our friends would wait for news of us and never know our fate. At last the pumping ceased, and I thought the leak must be stopped."

It was stopped, and the ship continued to sail south-south-east across the Atlantic. They sailed around the Cape of Good Hope, then north east along the South African coast. From there the ship reached the Indian Ocean, the Straits and the China Sea. The seas, sunsets and stars were beautiful but there seemed to be no end to them as the voyage went on and on. Spring turned into summer, summer into fall, and fall into winter. South of the Cape of Good Hope the cold was intense. The captain had a little coal stove set up in the cabin for the ship's passengers, where the Gibsons and Dr. and Mr. Fish popped corn and made molasses candy.

One night the cold was worse. "The barometer was falling, the wind was howling through the rigging, and a storm was brewing. In the night the mate came running to the captain's door. We heard him say, 'Man overboard, sir.' The captain bounded to the floor and ran on deck, ordered the ship put about, threw over a hen coop and other things, but it was dark as pitch and a terrible sea running. Soon the ship resumed her course and poor Jack was left to his fate. How sad we all felt. O, how we longed for a sight of land!"

After 80 more days of nothing but ocean sailing, the Gibsons were desperate to see land again. Finally, the clipper ship rounded Java Head and Angier came into view. Eliza described the glorious sight.

"With its green trees loaded with fruit, with its brilliant flowers lay before us. Scores of small boats came off with nude natives to sell all manner of tropical fruits, vegetables, monkeys, parrots, love birds, doves, cockatoos and canaries. We were becalmed there all day much to the chagrin of our captain, but to our great pleasure. We wanted to go ashore but the captain said we would go at our peril, for at the least breeze we would set sail. About dark a slight breeze came and we were off. But what a never to be forgotten day it was. Then we sailed through the Straits and felt the spicy breezes that blew soft o'er Ceylon's Isle."

Hong Kong

After long months at sea the ship finally dropped anchor in Hong Kong Harbor where it stayed for a few days. The ship was bound for Shanghai and the Gibsons for Foochow, so they said their goodbyes to the young missionary couple, the captain and crew. However, there was no regular ship travel to Foochow so the Gibsons had to rely on a ship whose captain was willing to take them.

After 3 weeks in Hongkong Otis heard of a freighter bound to Foochow. He went to see the Captain Josh Patten to ask for passage, but the captain was nowhere to be found. The first mate told Otis to find Mrs. Patten as she was actively involved with her husband's shipping business. Mrs. Patten was not helpful. She said that the ship did not take passengers because the cargo hold and every stateroom were filled with goods. He sighed and told her how disappointed his wife would be. To that she said, "Oh, is there a Mrs. Gibson? I have not seen a white woman for over five months. Why, yes, Josh can take you as well as not. I'll have a stateroom cleared out right away."

The Gibsons boarded the Neptune's Car for Foochow.

After a trip of two weeks they finally reached their journey's end in August 1855, almost one and a half years after their departure from New York City.

Once in China the Gibsons got to work. They and their co-workers, both white and Chinese established the first two Methodist Episcopal churches in East Asia. They also founded a boarding school for laymen and ministers, and Otis helped to translate the Bible into the local Cantonese dialect. The work was hard but God blessed it, and Chinese converts populated the churches and boarding school. Meanwhile Eliza bore two sons although tragically, one died as a small baby.

They were determined to live out the rest of their lives in the mission field that they loved. But after a decade in Canton Eliza's health was failing. They prayed and sought God's will for their lives. They decided that God wanted them to return to the U.S. and in 1865 they left for the country they had not seen in ten years. They had meant to work in China all their lives and had no idea what God wanted them to do now. They returned to New York, prayed and attended church, and tried to trust God.

And God was working. He was preparing the way to bring them to San Francisco, where they would continue the work they loved with the desperate immigrants who needed them most. Although they did not know it yet, the next phase of their work was starting with another American – Lucy B. Hayes, the former First Lady of the United States.

Founding of the WHMS

"Women's minds are as strong as man's — equal in all things and superior in some." (First Lady Lucy Hayes)

Former President Rutherford B. Hayes' wife Lucy was plain mad. She sat on the hard stone patio and for the third time read the telegram. "Elizabeth Rust at it again. Published story about your gift of large roll of butter from farm to luncheon. Paper caricatured gift. Do not blame them. Have you gotten over the chicken story yet."

Lucy's son Rud had telegraphed his mother about her over-zealous admirer's report in the local paper. Elizabeth Rust meant well but had caused a national furor over Lucy raising chickens to sell. Lucy raised chickens because she enjoyed owning a farm, but the press decided it meant that the Rutherfords were destitute. Citizens from all over the country sent telegrams and wrote letters offering to contribute to the former President and First Lady. The flap deeply embarrassed the dignified couple who in fact had no financial problems at all.

Elizabeth Rust was the Secretary of the fledgling Women's Home Missionary Society (WHMS) of which Lucy Webb Hayes was its first president. Later that day she wrote about Elizabeth to her best friend and WHMS vice president Eliza Davis. "The disagreeable report about my raising chickens to sell has nearly died out and now she has started another story."

President Rutherford had promised the country that he would only serve one term. Following the end of his four years he declined to run again, and the Rutherfords left the White House and moved back to Lucy's beloved Spiegel Grove farm in Fremont, Ohio. A lifelong Methodist, Lucy swung into action with the Woman's Relief Corps, her Sunday School class, and reunions of her husband's Civil War command. In her scarce leisure hours, she hosted visitors to the farm including her grown children's visits, and spent time with the farm's animals. (Not just the chickens.) To these responsibilities she reluctantly added the presidency of the Methodist Episcopal Church's Woman's Home Missionary Society.

She was initially drawn to the WHMS because it had begun its domestic missions outreach with the freed blacks of the South, who were living in deplorable conditions. Lucy's family taught her at an early age that slavery was an offense against God. Her father came from the slave-owning state of Kentucky. When Dr. James Webb inherited nearly 20 slaves from his aunt he moved the family back to Kentucky, promptly freed the slaves, and hired them to stay on with the family. He stayed to treat both whites and blacks who were suffering from a cholera epidemic. Tragically, Dr. Webb was infected along with his parents and brother. All four of them died leaving his wife Maria Cook Webb, three young children, and 20 former slaves. A family friend encouraged Mrs. Webb to put her family first and sell the freed men and women back into slavery. Mrs. Webb retorted, "I would sooner take in washing to support my family than sell slaves!" Mrs. Webb moved her entire household – including its black members -- up north to live near her family in the Free State of Ohio.

Despite her unfortunate series of articles, Elizabeth Rust and her husband, MEC pastor Dr. Richard S. Rust, were well-known home missionaries. The two headed up the American Missionary Association's (AMA) Freedmen's Aid Society that was founded to educate and aid freed slaves. The AMA's leadership was outspoken abolitionists before the Civil War and the AMA was one of the very few Christian organizations that employed both whites and blacks in prominent positions. The AMA sent teachers from the North and helped to found more than 500 schools and colleges for freed men, women and children. 5000 students would pass through these schools during the Reconstruction era alone. The schools trained former slaves in professions such as teaching and nursing -- a great work for that day when so many blacks lived in grinding poverty and with no education.

However, the Freedmen's Aid Society was concerned about the number of women and children who could not attend their schools. Most of these households were single mothers with no money or transportation. In the early 1870s the Rusts heard about the work that MEC members Mrs. Jennie Hartzell and her pastor husband Dr. Joseph Hartzell were doing with the freedwomen in New Orleans.

Jennie Hartzell was ministering to the women and their children by setting up community help centers and tiny local schools. She also added mothers' meetings to help the former slaves care for their children, offered classes in reading and writing, and established a mission school that taught the Bible. Many of the ex-slaves were practicing Christians but knew little about the Bible; and literacy and Bible reading were natural companions.

Jennie's work had started with home visitations – a brave thing for a sheltered white woman to do given the deplorable conditions in which the black families lived.

Elizabeth Rush immediately began publishing news about Jennie's work in the AMA and Freedmen's Aid Society publications. Then she did more: she invited the Hartzells to attend the 1880 General Conference in Cincinnati, Ohio. She believed that when the General Conference heard about Jennie's work they would approve the creation of the Woman's Home Missionary Society.

It was not easy for women to get official hearings without male support and Jennie had the backing of her own pastor husband and the ministers of their regional Louisiana Conference. But when the Hartzells reached Cincinnati prepared to speak, the General Conference never got around to voting on the matter. The next meeting would not be for another four years.

Never Give Up

But many people believed that the WHMS was in the will of God and were ready to help. Right after the General Conference ended, Dr. A. B. Leonard, the Presiding Elder of the Cincinnati District, spoke with the Hartzells. Dr. Leonard had a suggestion – instead of waiting another four years, schedule a meeting with the MEC women in Cincinnati. Jennie might find her answer there.

Jennie and Elizabeth set the meeting for June 8th in Trinity Church. The day turned stormy and the driving rain never let up. Despite the extreme weather 50 women showed up to the church to hear about the work with the freed slaves.

Elizabeth moderated the meeting and Jennie spoke, and at the end of it the women decided to start the organization themselves. They would call it the Women's Home Missionary Society which would "enlist and organize the women of Methodism in behalf of the needy and destitute of all races and nationalities in this country." Their very first outreach would be in New Orleans with Jennie Hartzell and her mission school.

The *Cincinnati Gazette* picked up the story and reported that the meeting concerned "the organization of a society having for its purpose the amelioration of the conditions of the freed-women of the South."

But before the newly minted WHMS could start their work in earnest, they needed a president who the men of the Methodist Church would take seriously, and who could hold her own against the existing MEC Women's Foreign Missionary Society, which was not at all certain it wanted to share its funding with a new women's missionary organization.

Elizabeth Rust's husband made a startling suggestion: ask Lucy Hayes Rutherford, a lifelong Methodist and the First Lady of the United States. The women hesitated to contact the great lady, but the Rev. Rust pointed out Lucy's faith, church activity, and her tireless efforts on behalf of the needy.

Still anxious about reaching out directly to Mrs. Rutherford, the women contacted Lucy's pastor. The pastor studied their materials, met with them and was convinced that the new organization was blessed by God. He contacted Lucy Rutherford and made the case, then let the women carry it the rest of the way.

But Lucy was enjoying her retirement from the White House and was reluctant to take on such a big responsibility involving speeches, organization, travel and fundraising. Her best friend Eliza Davis had already joined the new WHMS as a vice president and was convinced that Lucy should be president. On July 1880 she wrote to Lucy that the new organization had in fact voted Lucy in. She thought she should know "the action taken by the newly formed society here in making you its President. I think it is right to say that *I* am in no way responsible for even the least hint in that direction." Lucy then complained to Eliza that she was not good enough for such a responsibility, but Eliza firmly disagreed with her.

Lucy still did not decide to accept or reject the presidency. In November Eliza wrote Lucy again with a hint of asperity. "What are you going to do about being president of the Home missionary society? It is a great big idea (organize schools among poor whites, negroes, Indians & Chinese) and send women missionaries among them. I really believe you now have the opportunity of doing a really good thing by your name and position and good helpful judgment."

Lucy finally accepted the position with conditions on travel and fundraising responsibilities. Eliza delivered Lucy's acceptance to the women and wrote back with their reaction. "The 'Home Missioners' are duly and sincerely grateful - They accept the conditions of your acceptance of the presidency - but I shall expect to see you presiding at mass meetings and even making fervid and eloquent addresses!!! Women are moving now a days and there is no telling where it will stop."

The next General Conference officially accepted the new organization in 1884; 4 years after Jennie despaired at their refusal to hear about her ministry. She reported to the WHMS meeting that the General Conference after "ample consideration" (was there a shade of irony in her voice?) "adopted it as one of the trusted instrumentalities of the Church." She also said that the organization's responsibility was not only to white women and children. "We must add the just claims of the lately emancipated people and their posterity, of the Indians, of the Mormons, of the Spanish Americans, and the Chinese now within our borders."

Lucy served as president of the WHMS until her sudden death from a stroke in 1889. Her husband, former President Rutherford Hayes, survived his wife for three more years. His last words on earth were "I know I am going where Lucy is."

Lucy's friend Eliza Davis succeeded her and carried on the work of the WHMS. Within a few short years the ministry that began among the freed women and children in the South extended to Native Americans, Mormons, blacks and poor whites in the South, poor communities on the American Frontier, and to the Chinese immigrants on the Pacific Coast.

The Devil Came Down to Chinatown

The Devil Came Down to Chinatown

The Methodist Mission is Born

"If it is God, it will succeed." (Otis Gibson)

The WHMS didn't know it yet, but they were about to meet two of the people who would the most responsible for destroying the San Francisco slave trade: Otis and Eliza Gibson. After the Gibsons left China for the United States, Eliza Gibson's health improved. In 1868 the small family travelled from Moira, New York to a new assignment in San Francisco where Otis would serve as the superintendent of the MEC's Chinese Domestic Mission. This outreach ministered to Chinese immigrants in California, who were overwhelmingly men.

The Gibsons and their co-workers opened churches and missions throughout central California and Otis was active in the political arena. In 1850 Gibson spoke to Congress.

"The history of the 'Anti-Chinese Crusade' in California, during this Centennial year of American independence; the grounds upon which it has been waged; the character and spirit of its leaders and active agents; the methods of the campaign, the willful misrepresentations made concerning helpless and defenseless strangers who have come to us by special invitation; the criminal perversion of testimony given under oath; the ill-concealed effort to blacken the character of Protestant Missions and missionaries, in order to make a case against the Chinamen; the proud arrogance and assumption of superior virtue and morality by a class of men, many of whom, in daily life and practice, fall far below the average Chinaman -- all these things conspire to cause a blush of shame on the cheek of every intelligent Christian citizen who understands the case, whenever the subject is mentioned."

Gibson was fighting a rising tide. Most of the California press was stridently opposed to Chinese immigration and their purple prose inflamed the white population up and down the state. Gibson reported, "A large portion of the press of California devoted itself to fanning the flames of excitement. The people were daily treated to editorials and correspondence setting forth in exaggerated and highly colored phrases the vices and crimes of the Chinese people, the ruin caused by Chinese cheap labor, and the tremendous impending evils of further Chinese immigration."

A Divine Encounter

Yet for all the Gibsons' energy, there was an unreached population: the Chinese women and girls who were smuggled into San Francisco and who lived lives of misery and bondage.

The Gibsons were friends with the Rev. A.W. Loomis, a Presbyterian minister who was also active among the Chinese in San Francisco's Chinatown. Neither the MEC nor the Presbyterians had yet built missions to house rescued women and children. Even ministers who worked closely with Chinese men did not consider such a mission.

Loomis was in contact with the Ladies Protection and Relief Society at Geary and Franklin Streets. The Society was founded in 1850 by Protestant minister's wives to provide a temporary home and care for respectable white women whose men had died or abandoned them in San Francisco. Yet within a decade the emphasis of the Ladies Society had shifted to a more helpless group: children. Society literature stated that some of the children "are deserted by an abandoned mother, or a vagabond father, and are outcasts. Some come by sudden sickness of parents [or] death of a father or mother in poverty, rash speculation, the gaming table, or the curse of drunkenness." However, they only served white children -- until an 11-year-old Chinese girl with no name came to their door.

The Rev. Loomis was the first one to see her. The child came from Shanghai on a freighter bound for San Francisco. When she landed at the mail dock the inspectors asked for her name, origin and who had sponsored her to come. She would not say. The inspectors were puzzled. She had good manners and although her feet were not bound, she did not appear to be a peasant as were many of the immigrant girls. She might have come as a prostitute, or to serve a year or two as a *mui tsai* before being taken to a brothel. No one knows.

The inspectors sent word to Loomis, who arrived at the docks and took charge of the girl. But what was he to do with her? His wife had recently died so he could not bring an 11-year-old girl into his home. There were no orphanages that took in Chinese children and few of his congregation would agree to take in an unknown immigrant child into their families. Nor did Loomis want to turn her over to the Chinese since that placement would all too easily be a shortcut to slavery for the girl. So, the minister brought her to the only respectable orphanage he knew of that might take in a helpless Chinese girl -- the Ladies' Society home.

The matron met him at the door. She must have gazed at the minister and the solemn, silent child standing beside him. Did she hesitate? We do not know. What we do know is that the matron agreed to take in the immigrant child of a despised race and to raise her as one of the 80 orphans under her care.

By all reports the child thrived, largely due to an assistant matron and teacher named Mary McGladery who took the girl under her wing and taught her reading and the arts. The girl began to speak more Chinese and in a few months, began to learn English. But she still refused to say her name until one day when Miss McGladery asked her again. The girl hesitated and then said firmly in English, "My name is Mary McGladery." And she went by the name of her beloved teacher for the rest of her long life.

Because of his experience with young Mary, Loomis felt led to raise money for "some home or house of refuge" for orphaned Chinese immigrants and freed brothel workers. He told his friend Otis about Mary, and Otis met her where she lived in the Society orphanage in 1869. Otis never forgot that meeting and took it as a divine appointment. Otis and Eliza decided that just as Loomis was called to establish a Presbyterian home, God was calling the Gibsons to build an MEC refuge for the rescued slaves.

The Gibsons decided to start the Women's Missionary Society of the Pacific Coast to run the rescue work. The Gibsons sent out the call to attend a planning meeting and prayed that hundreds of concerned women would attend.

Only eleven came. But from this tiny start these eleven joined the Gibsons to found the Women's Missionary Society. The Methodist Mission building was already in operation and paid for thanks to Otis's tireless fund raising. Rental rooms were in the basement and the first floor housed three Chinese preachers who ministered at a small Chinatown chapel named the Good News Temple. The chapel and classrooms were on the second floor and the third floor was unused. The Society dedicated the empty floor as the "Female Department" on Christmas Day in 1870.

They waited for Chinese women to fill it… and waited. For 10 months the third floor sat empty.

The Story of Jin Ho

In hindsight this was not a surprise. Most of the brothel prostitutes were outright prisoners in the barred cribs. Even if they could escape, their owners had warned them that the whites would only pretend to help them, and would instead kill and eat them.

Then one night, Otis received a note from Captain A. Parker of the San Francisco Police Department asking him to come to the station. The note said that the police had rescued a young Chinese woman from drowning but that she refused to talk to a Chinese man. She said she would only speak with a

"Jesus man."

Otis went immediately to the police station. There he saw the woman, whom he described later as "a poor, wretched, confused, forlorn looking woman." She told him in Cantonese that her name was Jin Ho and kept repeating "Do not take me back to Jackson Street, do not take me back to Jackson Street."

She had escaped from a filthy brothel where she worked as an enslaved prostitute. She did not know where to go for help so she ran seven blocks to the black waters of the Bay and jumped.

But God had other plans for Jin Ho. A black fisherman fished at night so he would not have to deal with insults and violence from the white fishermen during the day. This man literally fished Jin Ho out of the water by hooking her wet clothes with his boat hook. He brought her onshore to the nearest police station, and they summoned Otis the "Jesus man" to help.

Otis and Eliza took her in to the Mission and cared for her. They found that her name was Jin Ho and that as with so many of these women, she had come from China on an American ship because she had been told she would marry a respectable merchant. However, the men who gave her passage had no intention of marrying her to anyone but put her to work in the hell hole on Jackson Street.

Gibson later told the rest of the story in his own words. "In six months from that time Jin Ho was so changed and improved that those who saw her at the Police Station did not recognize her. She remained about a year in the asylum, then did service in a Christian family, professed faith in the religion of Jesus, was baptized and received into the Methodist Church, and afterwards married a Mr. Jee Foke, a good substantial Chinaman, a member of the Congregational Church, with whom she is now living in peace and comfort, with none to molest or make her afraid. She is now clothed and in her right mind and enjoys a good hope of eternal life through Jesus Christ our Lord. Such was Jin Ho; and such is Jin Ho now, the first Chinese woman that sought refuge in the Asylum of the Methodist Mission."

Just a few days after Jin Ho's rescue a desperate 12-year-old named Ah Tai found her way to the Mission Home. She was a *mui tsai* who was going to be sold as a prostitute. The Gibsons took her in too, and Otis painted the Mission doorbell white so the refugees could find it more easily.

Otis reported the women's and children's desperate needs to the Methodist Church. "In plying their vocation, if these girls fail to attract, or refuse to receive company and make money, the old mistress beats and pounds them with sticks of firewood...starves them, and torments them in every cruel way...Case after case of this kind has escaped...and found refuge in the Methodist Mission House. They have sometimes come with arms, legs, and body bruised, swollen and sore, from the inhuman treatment received."

More women and girls were finding help at the Mission. But at the same time, white anger against the Chinese was stirring and was about to erupt in Chinatown.

The Devil Came Down to Chinatown

The Devil Came Down to Chinatown

The San Francisco Riots

"Everything was orderly until an anti-coolie procession pushed its way into the audience and insisted that the speakers say something about the Chinese. This was refused and thereupon the crowd which had gathered on the outskirts of the meeting attacked a passing Chinaman and started the cry, 'On to Chinatown.'" (Reporter Selig Perlman)

Most Americans resented the Chinese immigrants and the rescue missions were deeply unpopular because they pushed against the tide. When Otis Gibson published his great pro-Chinese work *The Chinese in America,* the press thundered against him and protestors burned him in effigy. Statements like these shocked working-class Americans:

"The doors of our country are open equally... We have room for all. Ours is the 'land of the free, and the home of the brave.' The oppressed and down-trodden from all nations may alike find shelter here, and under the benign influences of our free institutions, and of our exalted faith, with the blessing of Almighty God, these different nationalities and varying civilizations shall, in time, blend into one harmonious whole, illustrating to a wondering world the common Fatherhood of God, and the universal brotherhood of man."

Why was the American working class so hostile to the Chinese laborers and their defenders? The entire country was in the grips of the Long Depression that lasted from 1873 for the next ten years. The depression began in the east and many workers came west looking for work, many of them ending up in California's premiere city San Francisco. In a two-year period between 1873 and 1875 as many as 150,000 eastern transplants came to California looking for work.

In this atmosphere, hostility towards Chinese laborers worsened. The transcontinental railroad was completed, which released 9,000 Chinese workers into the tight labor market. Farm labor absorbed some of them but there was not enough work in the city to provide jobs for most of them. Many men in San Francisco were unemployed. There was no social safety net and people were angry.

Then in July of the year 1877, San Francisco exploded into riots against the Chinese immigrants. The spark was an outdoor rally led by the new Workingmen's Party of the United States. The Workingmen's Party was made up of radical socialists who had developed from the American branch of Karl Marx's International Workingmen's Association. They requested and received permission to hold a meeting on two adjoining vacant lots near San Francisco City Hall on the night of July 23. A few days before the meeting rumors ran rampant through the city. People claimed that the planned gathering would invade Chinatown and would burn down the Pacific Mail dock that served the freighters carrying Chinese immigrants.

However, the Chinese had no intention of lying down and dying. In the days leading up to the riots the Chinese Six

Companies wrote a subtle note to the Mayor. "We are not ignorant that self-defense is the right of all men; should a riotous attack be made upon the Chinese quarter, we should have neither the power nor the disposition to restrain our countrymen from defending themselves to the last extremity, and selling their lives as dearly as possible." In other words, were Chinatown to be attacked there would be blood... and it would not be Chinese blood.

That night the gathering began peacefully enough. It was a large meeting with about 8,000 people attending. The Workingmen's Party speakers did not attack the Chinese since their avowed topic was to show support for a railroad workers' strike in the East. Speakers railed against capitalism, business franchises and financial subsidies from the government to private parties.

But then an angry anti-Chinese group made up of young toughs from a local Democratic Party ward pushed their way through the crowd and demanded that the speakers talk about the danger of the Chinese to American laborers. When the speakers refused to do so, some other young men from the same ward spotted a passing Chinese man and attacked him.

The City Explodes

That was the flare that set the mob on fire. "On to Chinatown!" they shouted, and hundreds of men surged into the streets. As they headed for Chinatown they burned Chinese laundries along the way, and the mob split apart to find even more businesses to burn. Several hundred men made it to Dupont Street in Chinatown, eager to invade and burn. The San

Francisco police force beat them back, not for great love of the Chinese but because if Chinatown burned the fire may have spread throughout the city.

William Tell Coleman, an American business owner and founder of a citizen's law enforcement group, was present at the outdoor rally. He reported that it was a group of teenaged toughs who attacked the Chinese man near the rally that ignited the riots.

> "To Chinatown! Was now the cry, and off they ran up Leavenworth street, several hundred of them yelling like soldiers of Satan. On the south side of Tyler Street, above Leavenworth, stood some Chinese laundries; there the rabble bombarded, smashing doors and windows with bricks and stones. Thence they were driven by the police, but only to attack the unfortunate Asiatics in other quarters. The fiend-prince Maker [Satan] appeared to be in their urging to theft and demolition. Breaking into a corner grocery the mob-ites supplied themselves with bottles of liquor and canned eatables, after which they demolished a Chinese tenement on Geary Street, leaving it in flames. Fifteen other like places in that vicinity soon fell before them. Otis Gibson, of the Chinese mission, was stoned. [The Mission was stoned, not Gibson himself.] Meanwhile the police several times met and dispersed them with their clubs, until finally the rioters retired, leaving the city quiet for the night."

The Devil Came Down to Chinatown

The next day hundreds of men met and protested throughout the city, and at dusk they began to spread out. A full 500 of them decided to brave Chinatown again. Instead of torches they brought rocks and stones. Without the danger of fire, the police were not as determined to drive them back, and the mob surged into Washington Street.

Cries of "Otis Gibson!" went up and the mob converged on the Chinese Methodist Mission where Otis and Eliza lived. They threw rocks through the windows of the Methodist Mission and burned an effigy of Otis Gibson. Before anyone at the Mission was hurt, a combined force of California state militia, San Francisco police, and vigilante groups showed up to drive them out of Chinatown and off the streets of San Francisco.

The pro-order vigilantes distinguished themselves from the rioters by carrying hickory pickaxe handles as weapons. 4000 strong, they became known as the Pick-Handle Brigade and poured into the streets to help the police. Few of them held any sympathy for Chinatown but they guarded the Pacific Mail docks from the rioters who tried to set them ablaze. The Pick-Handle Brigade succeeded in protecting the docks and the firefighters who fought the fire, but a nearby lumber mill was set on fire and the men trying to put it out were attacked.

The battle raged from street to street between the rioters, vigilantes, and the police. California's Governor William Irwin telegraphed the Secretary of the Navy that U.S. soldiers might need to defend San Francisco's docks.

The riot lasted for two more days. Most of the damage was

in Chinatown where rioters destroyed twenty Chinese businesses, killed four people and caused more than $100,000 worth of damage -- a huge sum in those days. By some counts San Francisco's Chinatown was lucky – in 1871 a mob in Los Angeles murdered 18 Chinese immigrants.

The end of the riots did not quell the anti-Chinese sentiment. An Irish immigrant named Denis Kearney had been a member of the Pick-Handle Brigade but quickly turned to radical political protests. He was too much of a firebrand even for the Workingmen's Party, who rejected his application for membership because Kearney accused American workers of being shiftless and lazy. He founded his own organization called the Workingmen's Trade and Labor Union of San Francisco (later changed to the Workingmen's Party of California), whose charming slogan was "The Chinamen Must Go!" (Apparently the socialist Kearney never realized or cared about the irony of one immigrant shunning another over immigration.) Party politics were radical socialism with equal-opportunity hatred for both the Chinese and the rich. Kearny said:

> "We will send the Chinese home, distribute the land of the grabber, tax the millionaire, make a law to hang thieves of high as well as low degree, elevate the poor, and once more return to the simple virtue of honest republicanism.... When the Chinese question is settled, we can discuss whether it would be better to hang, shoot, or cut the capitalists to pieces. Either we must drive out the Chinese slave, and humble the bloated aristocrat, or we shall soon be slaves ourselves."

The Presbyterians

"The Chinese seem to occupy a superior position compared with other heathen nations, and yet alas! they are heathen." (Dr. William Speer, 1870)

During this unrest the Methodists were not the only mission standing in Chinatown. The Presbyterians were there as well. Presbyterian missionaries from the denomination were the first Protestants to formally evangelize Chinese immigrants in the Chinatowns along the west coast and the interior valleys of California. When missionary couple Dr. and Mrs. Speer returned from the mission field in China and settled in California, they were called to establish a mission in San Francisco's Chinatown. Dr. Speer urged the San Francisco Presbytery to work with the Presbyterian Board of Foreign Missions to establish the mission. The Board agreed, and the mission opened in 1852.

Both Dr. and Mrs. Speer spoke fluent Cantonese. Dr. Speer preached in Chinese to the men and the few women who came to the mission to hear about the Jesus Way. Within two years the Speers also founded the first Presbyterian Church in existence outside of China. The first four charter members were all Chinese converts who had attended Presbyterian churches in Hong Kong before emigrating to the U.S. The church was politically active, fighting against high mining taxes imposed only on Chinese miners and against the Exclusion Act. The Speers also founded a clinic in the mission. But as Dr. Speer aged he had increasing health problems. When he retired the banner passed to the Rev. A. W. Loomis and his wife.

Evangelism and church plants reached Chinese men and their wives and children. But the population they could not reach was the Chinese prostitutes who were virtual prisoners in the locked brothels. The movement to reach out to these women started with the Occidental Mission founding in 1873.

The Occidental Mission

A Presbyterian missionary named Mrs. John Gulick had served many years in Shanghai. In 1873 Gulick was in San Francisco to raise interest and money for an orphanage in Shanghai. Responding to the terrible plight of orphaned children and abandoned young women, eight of the women responded by forming a California Branch of the Women's Foreign Missionary Society to support foreign missions in China.

But the women could not raise enough money to fund the orphanage and the project withered. They felt that they were following the will of God and did not want to disband. They decided on a tangible domestic project. Interest in the enslaved Chinese immigrants began to stir. Pauline Robbins wrote, "In the early days, rumors were occasionally heard of the enslaving of Chinese women and girls. The Women's Occidental Board, organized in 1873, began a warfare to rescue these helpless girls."

The Board first rented a few tiny rooms in 1874 to serve as the Home until they could find a larger property near Chinatown. Sadly, the Mission Home's first matron was an unmitigated disaster. Harriet Phillips was supposed to teach the rescued girls how to cook and clean the house they lived in. It was a way for them to pay back the Mission for room, board and education, a way to build community among the girls, and a way to train them in housekeeping when they had a family of their own. But Harriett did not speak the language or understand the Chinese culture, and she did not care to. Her assistant matron was no better. The two women tried to do all the cooking and cleaning themselves and left the girls to their own devices. The matrons resented the girls and the girls resented the matrons, and Occidental Branch of the Women's Foreign Mission Society was ready to wash its collective hands of the whole sorry mess. Then Mrs. E. V. Robbins took the reins.

The Unsinkable Mrs. Robbins

Pauline Robbins and her husband had gone bankrupt in their hometown of Chicago, and moved to San Francisco to start a new life. She had been active in the Presbyterian Church and women's causes all her adult life, and as soon as they arrived in San Francisco Pauline joined the Occidental Branch of the Woman's Foreign Missionary Society. She was deeply interested in the Presbyterian Home and believed it was God's will that it succeeds, but the problems were serious.

Harriett and her assistant matrons had failed to supervise and educate the girls. They did not have a remote idea of the Chinese language or customs and did not care to learn, and the

Home was reeling towards disaster. When the Occidental Board stepped in to review the matrons, the women simply quit. Every Board member save one insisted that the home should be closed and the mission to the Chinese prostitutes abandoned as a failure. The lone holdout was Mrs. Robbins, who insisted that the home be kept open. The rest of the Board members asked her how that was going to happen. Pauline said that she didn't know but that God did, and they must leave the matter to her and Him. They agreed to let her try.

That very same day, Pauline found out that an American widow with four small children was stranded at the ocean dock. The young widow had no money and no friends on the West Coast and her situation was desperate. Pauline immediately left for the docks and discovered Mrs. Preston, a missionary to Canton whose husband had died there. She had had to bring back her young family to the United States but her extended family was back East.

Pauline promised to help, and then asked Mrs. Preston if she happened to know Cantonese. She did. Pauline went with Mrs. Preston and her four children to the Mission and asked if she might be interested in serving as matron. Mrs. Preston was quite interested and made the Home a success. The widowed missionary not only knew the language, she knew and respected the girls' native customs. The simple act of letting the girls cook Chinese food instead of insisting on an American diet cemented the relationship. And Mrs. Preston's bilingual children also helped to build relationships with the girls.

However, the Home's problems were not over. The Mission Home was rented in a rough area of town full of poor white workers who despised Chinese immigrants. Chinese men and women were frequent targets of verbal and physical attacks. The neighbors' prejudice extended to Mrs. Preston and her children, and she soon reported to the board that it was not safe for her, her children or the Chinese girls to stay by themselves without bodyguards. Again, the board voted to close the Home, and again Pauline Robbins was the sole holdout. She asked for more time.

Despite their financial difficulties in Chicago, she and her husband still lived comfortably. They were renting a fashionable home in a good part of town. That evening over supper she astonished her husband by saying, "Let us change our boarding place. I want to go and live a little while in the home that Mrs. Preston keeps for Chinese girls."

He was a businessman who worked with wealthy San Franciscans and was probably not enthusiastic about going to live in a mission home in a rough neighborhood. But Pauline explained why she believed this was God's will. To Mr. Robbins' everlasting credit, she persuaded him. They lived as boarders at the Home for several months. Their sturdy presence calmed the neighbors and the immediate danger passed.

But it was clear that the largely white neighborhood would never accept the Home, and the rented house was too small anyway. In 1876 the national Presbyterian Foreign Missions Board decided that an outreach to the immigrant Chinese fell under the category of foreign missions. In 1876 the Board gave the California group a generous gift of $5000 to establish a domestic ministry in San Francisco's Chinatown. Mrs. Robbins wrote about this time:

> "This western door had opened to the coming of strangers from China; to the people from a nation great with possibilities… The Chinese women have been brought here in their helplessness, their slavery, and their innocence. The traffic in them has been a cruelty and our Board felt it a duty to suppress it if possible, and to rescue the captives."

The Board requested additional donations for a new Home from Presbyterian churches all over the country. Eventually the Mission had enough money to buy a suitable property near Chinatown. They asked Pauline Robbins to lead the search.

Pauline and her committee found a 25-room house near Chinatown that they thought they could afford because the white couple who owned the building badly needed to sell it. They met with the landlady on the porch, but she was so incensed at the idea of Chinese living there that she spit in Pauline's face. The owners refused to sell it to the mission group.

However, the owners found no other buyers and were eventually evicted from the property for non-payment. The Presbyterian mission group could buy it after all. Yet even though the home was on the very border of Chinatown it was surrounded by white Roman Catholic neighbors who resented the Chinese intrusion. They were furious at its intended use. Neighbors bitterly complained, vandals struck the house, and one night a mob formed and threatened to tear down the building.

Neighborhood workmen refused to work on the house, so the women hired workmen from outside the neighborhood to remodel the interior. They did not explain what the building was for. When the interior was complete the group and their rescued Chinese girls moved from the rented apartments to the new home. One of the moving men was an African American. Ironically enough, when he saw the Chinese girls he simply quit work saying, "I can't stand that."

Eventually the work was done, and the attractive Home was ready for the move. Yet incredibly, a group of male ministers met with the Board and suggested that the women sell the new Home for Chinese Girls and give the money to the church to buy a new Synod headquarters. The pastors thought perhaps a floor of the new headquarters might be used for the women's work. The women thought perhaps the ministers were insane. The proposal did not pass, and the matrons and girls moved into the lovely new Home.

The neighborhood was much improved and closer to Chinatown. Yet the Chinese slave owners did not like the missions interfering with their profitable slave traffic. The powerful Tongs were to blame for a wave of violence that would threaten the Mission's existence.

The Rise of the Tongs

"Let highbinders and all other sons of Chaos beware, that whether they belong to the Chee Kung Tong, the Mafia, the Clan na Gael or any other such association, this country is no place for secret tribunals, bloody plots and dark conspiracies; and if they will defy our laws, assassinate innocent people, and tamper with our courts of justice, they will do so at their peril; for a long-suffering but outraged community may rise some day and cast them forth with all other devil-possessed things into the Gadarean abyss." (Rev. Frederic Masters)

The Tongs were Chinatown's homegrown gangs. They effectively ruled criminal activities in Chinatown and were key to keeping the Chinese brothel slave trade alive. On May 15, 1894 the *San Francisco Chronicle* published an article on the work of the Tongs.

"The crack of the pistol last night had a far more ominous sound to the police than the report of a murderer's revolver. It convinced them of the correctness of their suspicions, held for the past week, that another war of the Tongs, or Chinese highbinders, has commenced and once started there is no telling where these feuds will end. For several weeks the Tongs all over Chinatown have been playing war music in their rooms, and while the shrill, saw-like sound of the Chinese fiddle and the squeak of the Chinese clarinet are common sounds in the Mongolian quarter, those familiar with Chinatown and Chinese ways know that when the music continues until late in the night . . . some lodge of Tongs is at work offering sacrifices to the god of war and preparing to wreak vengeance upon its enemies."

"Offering sacrifices to the god of war" was not mere hyperbole – the Tongs were modeled after the Triads of China, the deadly gangs of the mainland that bowed before the statues of war gods.

The word "tong" is innocuous enough. It simply means a gathering place or hall. However, the "Tong" came to denote secret criminal societies that reached their zenith in San Francisco's Chinatown before the 1906 earthquake finally crippled the Tongs' criminal businesses.

From Benevolent Society to Criminals

The Tongs began as benevolent societies for mutual protection of Chinese immigrants, which explains why their translated names read like a Chinese heaven: The Peace and Benevolence Society or the Society of Pure Upright Spirits. The fact was that they had little money to help their various members, so they looked for ways to make fast money: gambling, opium, prostitution, and "protection" fees forced from Chinese merchants. Before long the Tongs devolved from a benevolent association to purely criminal and violent gangs.

Their street solders were called *boo how doy,* or as Americans called them the "highbinders." The word "highbinder" first appeared in the press in 1806 to describe Irish criminals and highway robbers. (Some journalists used the word to describe errant congressmen, as in "the highbinders of Congress.")

Eventually the word came to mean the foot soldiers of the Tongs: the enforcers, the "hatchet boys." These street soldiers battled each other at their Tong bosses' will. They rarely attacked policemen, preferring to bribe them to look the other way.

Historians estimate that there were anywhere from 19 to 30 Tongs at the height of their power, with about 50 to 1500 members apiece. It was common for men to belong to several Tongs at once. The 1880s and 90s were a particularly violent period, so much so that the time referred to as the Tong Wars. Highbinders fought each other through the alleys and streets of Chinatown, on fire escapes and on rooftops. Many of the quarrels erupted over the slave trade. For example, one Tong tried to take over a rival Tong's brothels, or punished a Tong member who had bought a girl but had not paid her full price.

The Tongs were infamous for issued assassination orders. In one case, the Chee Kung Tong of Victoria, Canada, were active slavers up and down the West Coast. A local missionary to Victoria's Chinatown named the Reverend J. E. Gardner actively rescued enslaved Chinese girls, and the Tong issued a kill order. Mr. Gardner found out on time and got police help to find the would-be assassin, a highbinder named Lum Hip. The man was an elite fighter of the Tong. In the hotel room where they found him were stashed the tools of his trade: chain armor, knives, a revolver and a hatchet. The man also had a business-like document in his pocket. It was signed by the Victoria branch of the Chee Kung Tong and dated July 2nd, 1887. The business-like contract is chilling.

> "To Lum Hip, Salaried. It is well known that plans and schemes of government are the work of the learned holders of the seal; while to oppose foes, fight battles, and plant firm government, is the work of the military... You, Lum Hip, together with all other salaried soldiers, shall act only when orders are given; and without orders you shall not act... When orders are given you shall advance valiantly to your assigned duty, striving to be first, and only fearing to be found laggard. Never shrink or turn your back upon the battlefield.

> "You shall go under orders from our director to all the vessels arriving in port with prostitutes on board, and shall be on hand to receive them. Always be punctual; work for the good of the State (the society), and serve us with all your ability. If, in the discharge of your duties, you are slain, this Tong undertakes to pay $500.00 sympathy money to your friends. If you are wounded, a surgeon shall be engaged to heal your wounds; and, if you are laid up for any length of time, you shall receive $10.00 per month. If you are maimed for life, and incapacitated for service, you shall receive the additional sum of $250.00; and a subscription shall be opened to defray the expenses of your passage home. If you shall exert yourself to kill, or wound, any one at the

direction of this Tong, and are arrested and must endure the miseries of imprisonment, this society undertakes to send $100.00, every year, to your family, during the term of your incarceration."

The Rev. Frederic Masters who worked closely with the Methodist Mission in San Francisco wrote extensively about the highbinders. He pointed out that the Tongs are a way of life among the Chinese and that many young men are lost to the highbinder societies. For example, becoming a Tong highbinder or hatchet boy was not just a modern gang initiation. The men were not only initiated into the Tong but into the worship of the god of war. In his article "Among the Highbinders" Masters described the detailed initiation of the criminal Triads in mainland China. The Tongs imitated the Triad ceremonies. Masters wrote, "The initiation of 'hatchet boys' is simpler than that of the triads above described. The candidate kneels before the god of war, crossed swords are laid on the floor in front of him, and a naked sword is held over his head while he swears fidelity and obedience to the directors of the Tong."

The *Daily Alta California* described the Tongs and highbinders in an article dated March 26, 1873.

"Last evening four Chinamen were arrested by officers Ward and Rodgers, and charges of riot, discharging firearms and malicious mischief. Their object was to obtain possession of a Chinese married woman on Stout's alley, who is indebted to them for a small amount. For the purpose of intimidating the persons in the house they fired off pistols, collected a crowd, and armed with hatchets and bars, went into the house for the purpose of demolishing the furniture and then kidnap the woman."

The Tongs' role in the slave trade was highly profitable. They bought and sold women, owned brothels, and levied weekly "taxes" on the prostitutes working in their territory. The Mission workers – or the "Jesus women" – were constant thorns in the Tongs' side.

Normally the Tongs would have resorted to physical violence first, but threatening white women would be sure to have all the force of the law down on their heads. Where the Missions were concerned the Tongs tried bribery first and then, when that did not work, court battles. They still tried to intimidate the Mission women, such as planting a stick of dynamite at the Presbyterian Home. The threat was real: the Hop Sings Tong was particularly enamored of dynamite and once tried to blow up the headquarters of a rival Tong.

Kidnapping was also an ever-present danger. Every Sunday the workers and girls from the Presbyterian Home walked to church services at the Presbyterian Chinese Church a few blocks away. The Home workers all carried loud police whistles in case the highbinders attempted an attack, and on more than one Sunday those whistles shrieked and policemen came on the run to protect the little column of women.

Highbinders even threatened to assault the Home itself and force rescued girls back into prostitution. The Home often received threatening letters and notes. One time a stick of dynamite was thrown onto the Home's front porch. Another time they found a cache of explosives planted in the building with sufficient power to level the entire block.

This was no empty threat by the Tong. In January 1884 *The Alta California* breathlessly reported an attempted assassination of a white prostitute with dynamite in an article entitled "A Dreadful Deed." The would-be victim entertained Chinese customers, an act that threatened the Tongs' ownership of the Chinese brothel trade. The woman's rooms exploded. An Officer Parrott investigated the wrecked rooms and found a piece of ragged fuse about three inches' in length.

As time went on and the Tong Wars took more and more Chinese lives, both Chinese and white American forces attempted to stop them. The politically powerful Six Companies had warred against the Tong for years in the courts, but increasingly draconian federal laws had worn down the Six Companies' power. In the 1890s a new force was formed with policemen who were not in the Tongs' pockets, Mission rescuers such as Donaldina Cameron, and Chinatown dwellers who had had enough of Tong violence.

The California press and national press was also increasingly interested in San Francisco's Chinatown and reporters wrote hundreds of articles condemning the Chinese slave trade. Even Americans who were prejudiced against the Chinese -- most Americans -- were sympathetic towards the slave girls and angry that the trade was happening in the United States. This impetus gave the legislature the will to enact new laws meant to diminish the slave trade and opium dens.

Powerful Chinese figures did their part including the Six Companies and the Chinese Consul Ho Yow. The police created a detailed map of Chinatown's crime scenes. The buildings that sported the highest crime rates were usually Tong headquarters and living quarters, and special police squads mounted raids on the suspect buildings.

These activities helped to blunt the power of the Tongs, but it was the great earthquake and fire of April 18, 1906 that would cripple them forever. Tongs still exist today but never regained their hold on criminal activities in San Francisco.

Miss Margaret Culbertson Strikes

"We were between the Scylla and Charybdis -- danger on both sides. Our missionary, Miss Margaret Culbertson, went into the conflict undaunted." (Pauline Robbins)

In the Tongs' heyday they feared no one -- except rival Tongs and two women: Margaret Culbertson and her successor Donaldina Cameron of the Presbyterian Home.

Miss Margaret Culbertson was a sharp thorn in their side for 16 years. Margaret worked as a teacher and director of the Presbyterian Home. She began rescuing girls before the rescue work was popular, at times carrying on a virtual one-woman battle to free Chinese girls held in slavery. Margaret wrote extensively and kept a journal of her rescues and her girls. Margaret wrote down Chun Loie's story on March 25, 1892, hurried misspellings and all.

"I received word in the afternoon that a little girl about 9 years old at the N.W. corner of Clay & Dupont Sts. was being badly beaten. I got the police went to the house and brought her to the home -- she was in pitiable condition, two cuts from a hatchet were visible on her head -- her mouth, face and hands badly swollen from punishment she had received from her cruel mistress." Margaret and the policeman rescued the little girl and took her to safety at the Home.

The Story of Yute Ho

One day in 1882 a fifteen-year-old girl named Yute Ho rushed onto the porch of the Presbyterian Home. She was wounded from multiple beatings and shaking with fear. The Mission women took her in, put a blanket over her and fed her. Their interpreter Chun Fah listened to the teenager's story and translated it for the Americans. It was a story they had heard too many times before.

Yute Ho was born an unwanted girl in a starving village in Canton. Such babies were often exposed and left to die, but this family did their best to raise her. Her father worked whatever poor fields he could find. But her father died before Yute Ho's tenth birthday, leaving the family destitute. Shortly thereafter a sophisticated Chinese woman arrived in their village. This woman told them that she had immigrated to California, to the famed Gold Mountain, and had come back to lead other young girls to the promised land. If Yute Ho's mother would release the child, then this woman would see that she married a rich Chinese man in the far-off land of California. Gold changed hands and the woman took Yute Ho. The child would never see her mother again.

The woman was a liar and a slaver. She took the ten-year-old to the Hong Kong docks and paid for the child's passage in a freighter. The little girl traveled in the hold with other Chinese women who were coming to California hoping to locate their immigrant husbands, or with the hope of finding and marrying a respectable husband themselves. Several of the younger girls had been kidnapped or bought from their parents like Yute Ho had been. Few of them would see their homes again.

Young Yute Ho was not immediately married or brought to the brothels, but was sold as an indentured servant. She worked hard and ate little, and when she was 15 she was sold to a middle-aged Chinese pawnbroker for $300. He turned out to be little better than the brothels because he regularly beat her. Believing that he would kill her, Yute Ho waited until he had gone out to a gambling den, then escaped the little house and ran for safety to the Presbyterian Home.

However, her owner was not about to lose his slave or his investment of $300, not a small sum in those days. He knew that he could not bribe or influence Margaret Culbertson, but he thought he might have a chance with the Occidental Board who administered the Home, and with the Board president Mrs. Browne. The owner bought an armful of beautiful Chinese silk and headed across the Bay to present his greetings to the good lady, and would she put in a good word for him at the Mission?

Mrs. Browne most emphatically would not, and insisted that he and his Chinese silk leave at once. His next plan was to poll the entire Board, hoping that they would force Margaret to release Yute Ho to him. He did not come alone. On the day of the Occidental Board meeting he gathered his troops: a group of prominent Chinese merchants and one Colonel Bee, an American lawyer with a busy practice in Chinatown. The merchants arrayed themselves in stunning Chinese robes and presented themselves before the good ladies of the Board to plead the "husband's" case.

The Board knew that he was coming and brought along Yute Ho so she could answer him directly. When the impressive Chinese contingent appeared, Yute Ho came out as well. The girl was shaking so hard she could barely walk, and two mission workers supported her. When the pawnbroker saw his former slave, he broke into rapid Chinese, which was immediately translated for the Board. He assured his young wife/slave that if she returned he would treat her kindly. The terrified girl refused to go with him, but the merchants who had accompanied the pawnbroker insisted that she must go. Colonel Bell then added his rich tones to the cacophony of voices, all demanding that the girl rejoin the man who called himself her husband.

At this point Mrs. George Barstow, the socially prominent wife of a respected judge, stood up. Her voice rose over the babble and she spoke firmly to the pawnbroker, his friends, and his lawyer. "If this girl elects to become an American citizen, the privilege should be accorded her, and there is no law in the land to compel her to a life of servitude."

Shocked, everyone in the room stared at her -- including the members of her own Board. Citizenship for a runaway peasant girl, a foreign slave? According to Mrs. Barstow, yes.

The pawnbroker and his contingent beat a retreat, but the man wasn't done yet. His next salvo was through the courts. The pawnbroker made a formal complaint to the court, who issued a summons to Margaret Culbertson. Margaret was to forthwith bring Yute Ho with her to San Francisco's Law

Library the following Saturday evening for a hearing with a judge.

Margaret was no fool and had no intention of bringing Yute Ho to an informal court where the girl could be easily be whisked away. Instead Margaret brought her friend the Reverend Kerr of the nearby Chinese Presbyterian church.

Colonel Bell was there as the pawnbrokers' lawyer. However, he had been on a weekend drinking binge and so was thoroughly drunk in front of the judge. The proceedings began anyway.

Margaret stated that the hurried summons had not required her to bring Yute Ho with her. In fact, she said, she and Reverent Kerr had not even known what the summons was for.

The judge was skeptical but was also thoroughly unimpressed with the drunken lawyer. He refused to force Yute Ho to return to her husband but also ordered that the girl could not remain at the Presbyterian Home during the court case. He remanded the teenager to the respectable house of the Chinese Consul-General to wait until the case was decided.

Margaret agreed, but the next day when she brought Yute Ho to the Consul-General's house a man answered the door. Margaret insisted that she see a wife or housekeeper before leaving the girl there. When she was told that no woman resided in the house, Margaret outright refused to leave her there. The Vice Consul-General was visiting the home and came to see what the fuss was about. The distinguished man assured Margaret that Yute Ho could stay at his house instead with his wife and daughters. Margaret took Yute Ho to the Vice-Consul General's house. The terrified girl screamed for Margaret not to leave her there. Margaret assured her that she would be safe at the Vice-Consul's home and that she would soon be able to return to the Presbyterian Home.

Margaret, her staff and the Board members spent the next several days in prayer for Yute Ho. Margaret later reported that as she prayed alone in her room, she clearly heard God's voice. She recognized the words from Ephesians 6:13: "And having done all, to stand."

The court hearing resumed within a few days. Yute Ho did not appear. Had Yute Ho been living at the Presbyterian Home, Margaret would not have brought her to court. She had learned through bitter experience that it was all too easy for court to simply turn girls over to their owners. However, since Yute Ho was living at the Vice-Consul's house Margaret was uneasy that she was not appearing at court. Had the Vice-Consul been persuaded to turn her over to the pawnbroker?

The owner was working overtime trying to prove his good name and suitability as a husband, and had collected character references from Chinese and American business associates. If Margaret Culbertson and the Board had not seen the girl's injuries for themselves, they might have been persuaded. They had seen her wounds from beatings and they were more determined than ever not to let Yute Ho fall back into her abuser's hands. But they needed help, for even though the women who sat on the Board were prominent in San Francisco society, the testimonials from white businessmen were very persuasive.

On the final day of the court case, retired Judge Barstow joined his wife Margaret, her fellow Board members, and several rescued Chinese girls from the Home. Neither Yute Ho nor the pawnbroker was in court that day. Had she already been turned over to the man?

The pawnbroker's attorney was in court, but he was drunk again. Slurring his words, Colonel Bell asked for a continuance from the presiding judge. Before His Honor could reply, Judge Barstow leapt to his feet from his chair in the gallery. He thundered, "Your Honor, I demand that this court issue an order at once remanding Yute Ho to Miss Culbertson's care. There is no doubt in my mind but what there is a deep-laid purpose in the continued non-appearance of this child."

The presiding judge agreed with his distinguished colleague and issued an order that not only should Yute Ho appear at the next court hearing, she should be brought back to the Presbyterian Home in the meantime. The Board ladies marched straightaway to the Vice Consul-General's house where they found Yute Ho safe but panic-stricken. The girl clung to Margaret until they reached the Home safely.

A few days later the Board members, Margaret, her Chinese girls, and Yute Ho all attended court. The pawnbroker and his tipsy attorney never appeared. They sent a message to the judge that the pawnbroker had dropped the suit. Yute Ho was free.

The Story of Ah Kum

In another case, a Chinese slave was frantic to save her

daughter. The woman was enslaved to an upper-class merchant named Ah Ong. She sewed Chinese clothing for him to sell in his shops. The young woman had a six-year-old girl named Ah Kum who may or may not have been the merchant's daughter by his slave. The girl was small and frequently sick from malnutrition, which distracted the mother from her sewing. The angry merchant threatened to sell the child. At the mother's horrified response, he accused her of winning a large amount of $300 from gambling, and that she had to give him that money or he would sell the little girl.

After he had gone the young mother took her daughter and fled for the safety of the "Jesus women" at the Presbyterian Home. Margaret Culbertson and her mission workers listened to her story and took them both in. But Ah Ong had powerful friends in the Chinese community. Businessmen turned up every day at the Presbyterian Home's doors demanding to speak with the frightened mother, and each tried to convince her to return to her master. Finally, the Chinese Consul-General himself came with a procession of attendants. He was dressed in the long silken robes of China's aristocratic class. In front of the Mission workers he demanded that the young woman return to Ah Ong to preserve China's honor.

But Margaret Culbertson, no stranger to the rich and powerful, informed the august Consul-General that even he could not enforce Chinese customs on American soil. He knew that she was correct, so he softened his tone. He promised the young mother protection against reprisal, and that she and her child would have enough to eat and would not be sold again.

The escaped slave bowed low to him as tears dripped

down her face. The woman was from a culture that obeyed authority, where women were deeply subservient to men, and where a peasant and slave would never dream of disagreeing with the powerful Consul. But she displayed the immense courage that she showed when she fled with her ill child to the Presbyterian Home. She told the great man that she had spent six years with Ah Ong and knew him better than anyone else. She knew beyond a shadow of a doubt that as soon as she and her daughter were returned to him, her daughter would disappear or die and there was nothing anyone would be able to do to protect them. If the Presbyterian Home would accept her and little Ah Kum, there they would stay.

The Consul-General withdrew and Ah Ong dropped his suit. The Sunday school children of Grace Methodist Church raised support for Ah Kum's education, and she and her mother were finally safe. Years later the Home hosted Ah Kum's wedding to a fine Christian man.

Dreadful Deeds

Even children were pulled into the life. Immigrant girls younger than 12 or 13 would serve as indentured servants to pay back the cost of their passage. Some Chinese families honored their agreement with the girls and families in China by releasing them at age 18 to a decent husband or respectable profession. But many of the families did not treat these servant children well, abusing them in the home and selling them into prostitution when they turned 14.

Margaret and the Home rescued many of these children from their masters. She wrote that of all the stories she publicly told of these frightened children, she could multiply them by a hundred and still not reach the end.

One little girl's job was to sew from 7:00 in the morning until 1:00 the next morning. If she fell asleep she was cut and burned, or her eyes were propped open with sticks. When she came to the mission the volunteer doctors immediately went to work on her damaged eyes.

Another 8-year-old was terribly treated by her Chinese mistress, who was a bound-footed woman in charge along with her husband of a brothel on Dupont Street. A white acquaintance of the family was so horrified by the little girl's treatment that he himself rescued the child and brought her to the police, who immediately called in mission workers to witness the child's injuries. With the help of an Officer Holbrook, Margaret Culbertson went to the mistress's home and had her arrested.

The child's injuries were so horrible that Margaret immediately took out letters of guardianship. This was the Mission's common procedure in these cases so that the girls and women they rescued could not be legally taken back by their former owners without a trial. Margaret took the injured child and went before the Judge so His Honor could see the girl for himself. He immediately issued the requested letters and the slave owner came to trial. The Tong was active behind the scene and although the woman pled guilty she was only fined thirty dollars and released. But at least the girl was safe and eventually recovered from her injuries.

Death of Miss Culbertson

Another way that the Tongs kept control of their girls was to tell them that if the "white devils" got hold of them they would be imprisoned, tortured, and eaten by white cannibals. The young women were panicked and would often fight a rescue attempt thanks to their terror. The Presbyterian Home was not the only organization to experience the effect of the lies; the Methodists did too. In 1901 Mrs. Kate Lake participated in a rescue with local policemen. They went to a brothel on Sullivan Alley to rescue an underage girl named Yee Yow from prostitution. It was a violent scene: the mistress of the brothel hit Kate and the 15-year-old Yee Yow fought and screamed all the way to the Mission. She refused to eat, all because of what her owners had told her about the white devils and their poisoned food.

At the Presbyterian Home, an aging Margaret Culbertson tried to comfort a terrified young prostitute who had been brought by police. The girl kicked Margaret in the stomach, doing major internal damage. Margaret never truly recovered. She tried to continue her work but was in constant pain and weak, so in June 1897 the Mission decided to send her back east to live with her sister to recuperate and regain her health. They wanted her to return; the only possible successor on staff was a very young and inexperienced Donaldina Cameron. The Board wanted their legendary Margaret to come back to them. But Margaret did not survive the trip home. She died after a train journey to Avon Springs, New York. A local newspaper account related the story and its aftermath.

"Miss Culbertson died a martyr to the cause which had absorbed the labors of her lifetime. The last illness and death were caused by a kick given her by rescued slave girl. Brutality begets brutality, and some of the girls brought into the mission from the dens of Chinatown behave more like wild beasts than human beings. Terrible tales are told the wretched little creatures by their masters about the mission and the desire to implant wholesome horror at the place in the minds of the slaves."

The Church at Home and Abroad magazine wrote a fuller report on Margaret's life and death. The stark title read "Death of Miss Culbertson."

"At Avon Springs, N.Y., July 31, 1897, Miss Margaret Culbertson, of San Francisco, CAL., while en route to her childhood home, passed to rest. Margaret Culbertson was born and grew to womanhood in East Groveland, western New York. In 1878 she became connected with the Presbyterian Home in San Francisco, California, under the auspices of the Woman's Occidental Board of Foreign Missions and from that time until her death she stood a unique figure in that noble work.

"The large family of Chinese women and children at the Home, from which was carried only few days before her death, mourn as for a mother, and in the Christian homes in Chinatown and other cities at this State there are many saddened hearts. Miss Culbertson was "mamma" to the family in the Home, and to the girls who have married and passed out to found Christian household of their own.

"By Chinese men she was esteemed and revered as probably no other woman has ever been on this coast. The following is the opinion of one laundryman, but stands for the whole of the Chinese population of our city. When disease had first fastened its talons on the heretofore robust frame he anxiously inquired for the admired missionary. He was told that she would soon be home, very much improved in health, when he exclaimed: 'Oh! That is good; I am so glad. If Miss Culbertson goes away nobody can help our girls. All good Chinamen say that Miss Culbertson, she is our good lady, no lady like her before, no lady after now like her. China people love her, she is not afraid, when some man comes, says, "Come help," she comes, she is all the same mother for China girls. I tell you, do not forget, if Miss Culbertson is sick, you get plenty of help, don't let her go away. Her mouth says no lie. What she says is all right; no one can find two Miss Culbertsons.'"

A memorial booklet at her funeral read "To the Memory of Miss Margaret Culbertson, Militant Saint and Sainted Warrior, Who at Peril of Life, Fought a Good Fight for the rescue of Slave Girls of California."

The Devil Came Down to Chinatown

Saving Bodies, Saving Souls

"All enquiring persons... naturally wonder and question what does the Occidental Board do with its yearly harvest of waifs gathered from among an alien and heathen people? What does the Home teach these children, and what finally becomes of them? Our first care is to educate and train them along the simplest lines of Christian faith and duty." (Donaldina Cameron)

The Christian missions meant to save these young women, both body and soul. Jesus taught them to do both. "Go and make disciples of all nations, baptizing them in the name of the Father and the Son and the Holy Spirit, teaching them to observe all that I commanded you; and lo, I am with you always, even to the end of the age." (Mt. 28:19-20). Jesus Christ also said, "Then the righteous will answer him, 'Lord, when did we see you hungry and feed you, or thirsty and give you something to drink? When did we see you a stranger and invite you in or needing clothes and clothe you? When did we see you sick or in prison and go to visit you?' The King will reply, 'Truly I tell you, whatever you did for one of the least of these brothers and sisters of mine, you did for me.'" (Matthew 28:19-20)

For all the danger of the rescues, saving the body was the easy part. Saving the soul was harder. Part of the problem was a clash of cultures. Christian missionaries had been active in

China for years and there were native Chinese Christians. But by this time most of the Christian missions were located on the coast of China. Few remained inland where the poor Cantonese families sold their girls into slavery.

In many cases, the enslaved girls' first introduction to Christianity was the mission women, whom their owners had taught them to fear. Even when the girls realized they were safe in the mission homes, Christianity was still a strange, new – and mostly white -- religion. One young woman honestly shared that "it gives me a pain to hear this Jesus Christ stuff."

The fact that most Chinese identified any white American or European as a "Christian" did not help either. Many of the kidnapped girls' first introduction to whites were British or American slavers. In fact, the British governor of Hongkong reported through official channels that the men of the British colony required large numbers of brothel prostitutes to keep them satisfied and willing to stay to help protect British interests. The fact that most of these women had been kidnapped or lured by false promises from poor provinces made no difference to His Honor. Hardly a good witness to Christ.

The Americans lacked these colony bases in Asia, but they made up for it by working with Chinese criminals to kidnap and lure women and girls from China and Japan and ship them to America's coastal cities, where they were quickly and profitably sold.

Some immigrant Chinese had been introduced to Christ through the missions in China. Others accepted Christ on

American shores. In time the Chinese church came to thrive in the immigrant community. San Francisco's Chinese Presbyterian Church was on Stockton Street in Chinatown. San Francisco's first ordained Chinese minister, the Reverend Nam Art Soohoo, lived nearby.

The Methodist Mission workers and girls attended church in the Methodist Home mission church that the Gibsons founded, close to the border of Chinatown. Three Chinese preachers lived at the mission on a different floor from the Women's Floor and worked at the small Gospel Temple *Foke Yam Tong*, located in the heart of Chinatown. Otis Gibson had founded this chapel, explaining that the mission house chapel was located too far from the crowded streets in central Chinatown, whose streets were filled with rambling residents who might visit a church if they were to pass one.

In 1874, Methodist Mrs. F. Burke reported to the Women's Missionary Society of the Pacific Coast that over the past year the Mission House housed 18 Chinese women and girls. Eight of the women were married to "respectable" Chinese men, five of them Christians. Eleven of the women and girls had accepted baptism and joined the Church. All the girls attended religious services at the Home: a Sunday morning prayer meeting led by one of the girls, a Tuesday evening prayer meeting led by one of their teachers, a Chinese language sermon on Sunday morning, Sunday school at 1:30 in the afternoon, and an evening Sunday School at 6:00 pm.

By the end of the year Mrs. Burke reported that 24 women and girls had now come to live in the Home and they had had to expand their living space to accommodate them. She proceeded to ask for more money to help support the growing number of residents, and concluded with this telling remark: "We promise to exert ourselves to the utmost to raise all the missionary money we can; but we have to fight against the prejudice, we are pained to say, of many within our own Church when we ask for means to carry on the work among Chinese women in this country. May God guide and abundantly bless us in this good work!"

Eighteen years later in 1892, an MEC missions report wrote about the Methodist Home Church. 1891 had been a difficult year but things were looking up. Although deportations and one-way trips back to China decreased their original congregation during 1891, nineteen new members joined the church, and more were coming every month.

"The earlier part of the year was full of trial and discouragement. A marked improvement in the congregations and a deeper interest in the preaching of the word has been noticed during the last six months. Never have we seen our church in as good a state or so many seeking after the truth as now. A revival is just now in progress that is working out astonishing results. Every Sabbath sees some new inquirer coming forward and declaring his intentions to lead a Christian life. Every night a class of ten or fifteen anxious inquirers met under the leadership of Brother Chan Hon Fan to study the Holy Scriptures. During the last month we have received twenty men and women on probation for church membership."

The mission report happily described a regular class meeting held on Sunday nights. Following the preaching service, the students shared their testimonies that had "a thrill and force that characterize a good old-fashioned Methodist love feast. So gracious is the influence pervading these meetings that some of our lukewarm members have been quickened into new life, while two backsliders have been converted and received again into the church."

The challenge was that most of the church members were very young Christians and did not know much about their new faith. This laid a heavy burden on the pastor and the few experienced laypeople in the church. The congregation also struggled with being located on the fringes of Chinatown, which made it difficult to get immigrants adults and children to attend the church school in the evenings. The bigger problem was the Exclusion Act. The report stated:

> "First, fewer immigrants come to the coast; second, those who do come have, for the most part, been here before, and have learned all the English they care to acquire; third, the anti-Chinese legislation, has unsettled the prospects of the Chinese in this country, who are beginning to doubt the utility of learning any more English than will serve their present needs. The Mission longs to accomplish greater results and secure a wider hearing for what is after all our great business, the preaching of the Gospel."

They never forgot their other important task: rescue. "In addition to our regular preaching and teaching much time has been spent by the superintendent in assisting the authorities to combat the Highbinder societies, the gambling dens, the traffic in slave prostitutes, and in exposing the fearful spread of opium smoking and the trade in the drug at this port."

Painful Prejudice in the Church

Presbyterian missionary Mansie Condit worked closely with the Society and the Chinese Women's Home and frequently visited women and children. She was especially popular among the children, who would repeat her name every time she came to visit. "Mansie! Mansie!" they would cry excitedly.

Mansie was not as popular with local and state politicians, who refused to let their wives and daughters have anything to do with the Chinese for fear of a political backlash. Mansie Condit wrote frequently about what she considered as sheer cowardice. She did not spare Presbyterian ministers either, who either tried to ignore the women's Mission work or actively opposed it. This poor attitude directly impacted the Society's ability to raise money for the work, which they often did by speaking in pulpits on at worship services. Some ministers simply did not invite the women to speak and others openly refused. At this point Society members strongly suggested a meeting with their regional Presbyterian Synod of the Pacific. Some ministers boycotted the meeting, but others came, and opposing groups hammered out a temporary truce.

A few of the ministers joined the work themselves: Dr. Loomis and Mansie Condit's husband Dr. I.M. Condit. Both Condits were active with the immigrant Chinese and Dr. Condit spoke fluent Cantonese. They frequently visited the Home and worked with both rescued prostitutes and the Chinese men who labored on the railroad and on California's rich farms. The Presbyterian publication *The Occident* reported on Mr. Condit's visit to Alvarado, California.

"Mr. Condit visited Chinese quarters on several of the ranches and in the village on Saturday and gave notice of the service. It was an inspiring picture to see our missionary standing under the willows surrounded by a score of these dusky men, to whom his words of invitation and sympathy spoken in their own Tongue seemed to come as rain in the desert. It seemed like Paul's work -- like the Savior's work-- of going about doing good -- of taking a stand between the souls of men and death."

The Devil Came Down to Chinatown

Chinese Women Speak

"I saw the money paid, and I was taken on the twenty-sixth of last month of last year and placed in her den. They forced me to do their bidding, but I cried and resisted. I did not want to lead this life." (Rescued Chinese prostitute)

We have very few accounts of the trade by the prostitutes themselves. The newspaper interview of Suey Hin and Ah Toy's fame are rare. Most of the prostitutes spoke no English and the brothel guards were vigilant in keeping away journalists and interpreters.

There are however a few accounts that the rescue missions collected over the years. The Rev. F.J. Masters reported such an account from a rescued girl. Speaking through an interpreter she said, "I am seventeen years old. I was born in Canton. When I was ten years old my parents sold me to be a domestic slave. A man brought me here, and he returned to China having sold me for five hundred dollars. I came to this country three years ago. My master wanted to take me to be his slave, but I resisted. I did not want to be his slave. He had one wife already."

Masters added that one Mr. Young of the Episcopal Mission had spoken to the girl's master, and was told that the master's wife had bought the girl for three hundred dollars.

Another mission report told a second girl's story.

> "I was sold for $2,970; was a slave in a place of
> ill repute; never a wife. I escaped by running to a
> more friendly Chinaman who kept me till night, and
> then disguised in his American clothes, I was taken
> to a hotel on Bush Street. My master traced me and
> sent a spy, who got me into a carriage; but then they
> tried to take me into a cellar on Pacific Street. I
> screamed so that the police took me from them."

Her story did not end there: she was released back into the
custody of her master who took her to the cellar and fed her
drugs to keep her quiet. Missionaries who found out about her
first escape searched for her, located and rescued her.

A third witness who ran away to the Methodist Mission
told a detailed story of how the highbinders worked.

> "I am sixteen years old; was born in Canton.
> My father died when I was two years old, and left
> my mother and me and a little brother with no one
> to support us. My mother worked hard as a
> seamstress, and I helped her when I got older.

> "When I was fifteen years of age arrangements
> were made for my marriage, and I was betrothed to
> a man in Hong Kong. I did not see him, as
> according to Chinese custom we do not see each
> other. This was on the tenth day of the tenth
> Chinese month of last year. On the first day of the
> eleventh month he came up to Canton again with a

woman. He sent the woman to see me and to tell me to get ready to go down to Hong Kong with him. I told him that I must wait till my mother came home before deciding. She urged me to go at once as my husband was waiting. I went reluctantly, but I thought she spoke true.

"We went down on the steamship *Hankow*. She took me to a house, where we had a room together; but I saw nothing of the man who was to be my husband. After six days the woman left me in charge of a man, who said I had not got to my husband yet, and that I should have to go on a steamer a few days' journey before I saw him. They said I was going to California. We went on board the steamship *Belgic*. When we got to Japan we did not get off the steamer, but went on; then I cried to go back to my mother. I cried all the way over.

"There was a man on board who all the time was teaching me what to say. He coaxed me to be quiet, and told me I would have a rich husband and a fine time in California. He said I was to say I had been to California before, and left a year ago. He said I was to tell them my husband was a ladies' bootmaker living on Jackson Street near Dupont, and told me if I made any mistake in my words, and made any fuss, there would be a foreign devil come and take me away to the devil prison, and I should never see my husband.

"On the third day of the twelfth month I

arrived in San Francisco; but it was not before the sixth of that month that I came ashore. On that day a white man [a customs inspector] came to where I was and called out my name and gave me a white paper, and I went on shore and they measured me. Then I got into a hack with one white man and one Chinaman, and they took me to a house near the court. I was there for several days. I answered all the questions satisfactorily. I swore that my husband lived here, and that I had come to join him.

"I went back to a family house; and the next day a slaveholder came to see me, and asked me if I would like to go with her and be willing to go to a house of ill-repute. I indignantly refused, and said I was going to be married in a few days. Then I got suspicious and began to cry; but they told me not to fear, that I was going to a nice place, and would have plenty of food and fine clothes and jewelry, and go to the theater and have a nice time. The man who brought me over said I must go, and so the money was paid and I was brought. One thousand five hundred and thirty dollars were paid for me.

"I saw the money paid, and I was taken on the twenty-sixth of last month of last year and placed in her den. They forced me to do their bidding, but I cried and resisted. I did not want to lead this life. They starved me for days, trying me where food was almost in reach of me, which looked so good. They beat me time and time, and threatened to kill me if I did not behave right. I heard of the Mission, and waited my opportunity to run, and so I escaped."

She made her way safely to the Methodist Mission.

The MEC Mission Marches On

"On Monday night an attempt was made to kidnap a Chinese prostitute from one of the brothels on Jackson Street, and once she was on the street, a scuffle ensued between her mistress and the man who was anxious to obtain possession of her.... At her own request she was taken to the Methodist Mission Home." (Daily Alta California newspaper)

Home missionary Mrs. M.G.C. Edholm wrote an impassioned article called "A Stain on the Flag" for *Californian Illustrated Magazine*, where she laid into the shocking San Francisco slave trade.

"It was generally supposed that slavery was abolished in the United States during the administration of Abraham Lincoln; yet, if the facts were known, as they will be to the reader of the present paper, there exists in this country, wherever the Chinese have obtained a foothold, a slavery so vile and debasing... In San Francisco, Los Angeles, New York and other cities where a local Chinatown prevails, women and children are sold to the highest bidder every month in the year, -- not merely sold, but imported for the purpose, agents being kept in China for this object; and until the Restriction Act went into operation they were doing a thriving, land-office business... the luckless Chinese slave... is selected, bought and handed over for use compared to which death would be a happy release.

"For years this system of human slavery has been going on. Good men and women, representing the various churches, have fought it unaided, but it rests today a stain upon the American flag -- a blot upon the national honor; and the object of this paper is to present certain aspects of the crime to the lawmakers of the country, and to ask how long such things can be in a country that avowedly offers a refuge to the oppressed of all nations.

"In the work of stopping the sale of women and young girls in San Francisco, the hotbed of Chinese slavery, especial credit is due the Presbyterians and Methodists, who have established homes for the rescue and education of these girls and women. The annals of these institutions rival Shakespeare for tragedy; and for dark, damning deeds they read more like the records of barbaric ages and heathen countries than those occurring under the full light of Christian civilization... the records of these two homes show that hundreds of little girls and women have been rescued from this slavery worse than death; and Miss Margaret Culbertson and Miss Houseworth of the Presbyterian Mission, and Rev. F. J. and Mrs. Masters, Mrs. Downs and Mrs. Ida Hull of the Methodist Mission... could a tale unfold that would amaze and horrify the world."

Life in the Mission

Despite life-threatening circumstances, daily life went on in both missions. As the Mission became better known, many policemen and judges chose to send arrested or newly rescued girls to the Missions rather than keep them in jail or release them into the hands of their owners. The Mission served as guardians for the children until they were 18 when they could leave to get married, find a respectable job, or even stay on with the Mission as staff and interpreters.

The older teens and adults who were not under arrest could leave when as soon as they wished. Some did and went right back into their owners' hands. But most of these young women stayed for at least a year for safety and an education. They were required to obey Mission rules and go to classes and church services. The girls attended Chinese reading and English reading and writing classes, sewing and cooking classes, and helped to keep the Mission clean. They sold their fine sewing work to help support the Mission and to help them support themselves once they left the Mission.

The Mission also offered a Sunday school for the children

under their care that was open to the Chinatown community. 60 children from Chinese Christian families related to the Home. An 1892 report on the Sunday school said, "to give these little native sons and daughters of the Golden West a Christian education is a duty which our Woman's Missionary Society cannot neglect."

The Mission was also deeply involved in helping the young women to make respectable marriages. If the suitor was an honest worker and not a member of a Tong, he could court a willing girl. If the girl was Christian, then the Gibsons only allowed a Christian Chinese man to propose. Couples would have to wait a year before marriage and the young man would pay her board at $5 a month. This was to ensure that the Tongs were not sending imposters who would pretend to marry the girl and then sell her back into prostitution.

More than one couple found each other first and then asked the Mission for help. Given the extreme rarity of marriageable Chinese women in San Francisco, it was not unusual for men to visit the brothels and find a girl they wanted to marry. The men could pay thousands of dollars to the slaveowners to free the girl, but that amount of money was not possible for the working men. In these cases, a man and his fiancée could ask the Mission for help. If the woman agreed to be rescued from her brothel, the Mission launched a rescue and brought her to the Mission. She was still required to spend the same year in the Mission as any other rescued woman, and her fiancé was required to pay $60 during the year for their fiancée's room and board. In addition, the men had to sign agreements that they would not make their wives into prostitutes or sell them to another party.

The Mission sometimes placed older girls in white Christian households to learn Western methods of household management. Unlike the *mui tsai* system, the girls were paid in addition to their room and board. The 1892 MEC missions report put it this way: "a number of our girls who are employed in families and are not only earning their living, but gaining a sense of independence and self-reliance, which as paupers fed and clothed by the mission, they could never acquire."

The work was not easy. In 1897 Laura Lee, a nineteen-year-old former resident of the Methodist mission, wrote to the mission director Margarita Lake to describe her duties in the Reeves household of Alameda, California. "I feel like Robinson Crusoe away out here, away from all my kind and loving friends, but I thought I would write to you to let you know that I am alive. I am getting along nicely, and am very much satisfied with my new home, because Mrs. Reeves and her children are all very kind to me. I am learning to cook, and when I come home again to you, I will show you how nice I can cook. I cooked breakfast last Saturday all by myself, and had it all ready in time for the children to start for school. Wednesday morning I cooked the mush and did not put any salt in it, but the lady said she used to do the same thing herself at one time. Tell Gum that I am having worse troubles than she has. I get up every morning at 6:30 and make the fire and cook the mush and make the coffee and set the table, and wake up Mrs. Reeves to cook the meat."

Still, Lee longed for her Mission home and church in San Francisco. "I went to church with Mrs. Reeves and her children, but the very minute the preacher commenced to speak I commenced to cry, because I felt homesick for my own church." However, she wrote that she was glad that Mrs. Reeves allowed her to study from the children's books each day after they came back from school.

Some mission girls resented their work as domestics. Marie Chan, another former Methodist mission girl, described her loneliness while working in the home of the Edmonds family. Writing to the newly married Margarita Lake (Garton) in 1910, Chan complained about her situation and expressed a desire to return to her former life in the mission home. "I am not used of working like this, so I am awfully lonesome. I feel as if I had lost all my friends. Because this place that I am working now is between Oakland and Berkeley. Berkeley is just as far as Oakland from here. I am sick and tired of Oakland and Berkeley. I wish I could find a job in the city. I am going to the country with the family, for three weeks. We are going next Thursday. I hate to go with them, but in the case of had to. I know I will feel very lonesome, because I don't like countries. I like cities. Countries are too lonesome for me."

Love Blooms for Ida Hull

The work at the Homes was often hard and dangerous, but it could be joyful too. Ida Hull was one middle class white woman who decided that her comfort was less important than the brothel worker's lives. By the time she was 32 years old, Ida Hull was widowed and had a 10-year-old son. The two traveled to San Francisco in 1892 where Ida joined the Methodist Home staff as a teacher. Her first assignment was to start a kindergarten and to head up home visitations, which is where she encountered many abused children and young women. She worked with them for the next 10 years.

Ida did marry again but her choice was not the one her friends and family expected. Chon Han Fo, who wrote the letter protesting Rev. Lee's support of the Exclusion Act, worked with Ida at the Methodist Chinatown church and the Mission Home.

Chan Hon Fan was happily married to a prominent young woman who was a Chinese mandarin's daughter. He too was of the mandarin class. He was trilingual in Cantonese, Mandarin and English and dressed in American styles. He had become a regularly ordained minister of the Methodist Episcopal Church. He and his wife had four children during the years on the road when he preached at Chinese churches up and down the West Coast. Needing some stability for their children, in 1890 they settled in San Francisco to work with the MEC mission church.

After 9 years in the city Fan's wife died. Fan took care of his four children while continuing to minister at the church, and Ida raised her son at the Mission Home. Two years later they admitted to each other that they were in love and wanted to marry. It was a radical – and in California, an illegal – decision. The couple traveled to Colorado where marriages between whites and Chinese were legal, but where white ministers often refused to perform them. Local MEC pastor Camden M. Cobern agreed to perform a church wedding, and the news was the leading story in the *San Francisco Call* of February 25, 1901. The article was generally sympathetic to the couple and bore the blaring title "CHINESE WEDS A WHITE WOMAN."

"DENVER, Feb. 25. — Chan Hon Fan, a full-blooded Chinese, and Mrs. Ida H. Hull, a white woman, both of San Francisco, were married here to-day by the Rev. Camden M. Cobern, pastor of Trinity M. E. Church, the largest church in Denver. They tried to get married in California, but the law was against them, so they traveled to Colorado, where there is no statute prohibiting the intermarriage of Chinese and Caucasians. Being married, they will return at once to San Francisco.

"According to the story told to Mr. Cobern, they have been in love with each other a long time. When Mrs. Hull's husband died in San Francisco a number of years ago she had a call to preach the Gospel to the heathen. She went into Chinatown, where she met Chan Hon Fan, who was engaged in the same sort of work, being at the head of a Methodist Chinese mission. He was educated in English, came from the mandarin class, wore the clothing of the white man, was queue-less and was a regularly ordained minister of the Methodist Episcopal church. After trying to get a license in San Francisco, they decided Colorado would afford them the relief sought. On arriving here yesterday, they went first to Sing Lee, a California-street laundryman, whom Chan Hon Fan had known in San Francisco, and then to Dr. R. F. Lemond, a well-known physician, whom they met last summer while they were taking the children of their mission on an excursion around the bay. Sing Lee and Dr.

Lemond used their good offices with the County Clerk and with the Rev. Mr. Cobern, and there was no difficulty in getting a marriage license or a minister to perform the ceremony. The couple disappeared immediately after being married. Fan is about 35 years old and his bride about 30."

In somewhat of an understatement the article concluded by saying, "The two were known to be quite attached to each other, but the announcement of their marriage comes as an overwhelming surprise to their many friends in this city."

The Devil Came Down to Chinatown

Aggressive Measures

"It is evident that the increasing demand for evangelistic work among the Chinese necessitates enlarged facilities for aggressive measures." (1892 MEC Missions Report)

During the early days of Mission rescues, the emphasis was on women finding their way to safety at the Missions. But the Tongs fought back, making it harder and harder for the prostitutes to get word to the missions that they wanted to be rescued. If a woman succeeded in escaping, the owners fought to keep them through the court systems. After a girl was rescued the slave owners forced her and the Mission into court. Facing their captors, many girls were so frightened they blurted out that they wanted to return to the brothel.

The Mission rescuers countered their strategy in response. Instead of only providing a haven for women who reached the Missions, the missionaries mounted rescue missions at the guarded brothels and became experts at using the court to keep the girls they rescued.

MEC rescuer Ida Hull put it like this. She said, "I don't use much tact -- tact isn't useful among the Chinese. A hatchet is more effective. Oh, I only use it to break down doors with," she laughed, "not on their heads, although sometimes if I were a man I should like to."

Will Irwin, a great American reporter, discussed the problem in the early days of the Presbyterian Mission under Miss Margaret Culbertson.

"Usually, the Chinese slave-woman in America enters bondage in China, being sold by her parents, seized as an orphan, or stolen. Today most of the slaves held in San Francisco are domestic servants; but at the time when Donaldina Cameron began her work, two out of three were held for immoral purposes. The free Chinese woman who chose such as life was the exception; the slave was the rule. In the complex, mysterious underground life of Chinatown, these slaves kept the place they had always held in China, with the exception that they were infinitely more valuable, especially after the passage of the Chinese exclusion act in 1882. In early days a slave was worth less than $1,000. After 1882, the price was doubled. Now, with the entrance still further restricted, the market price for a girl of fourteen is about $3,000, for a baby, $2,000." These sums are in the currency of the late 1880s. They would be 10 times that today.

""This is for the grown girls. Soon the missionaries found that they could not count on keeping even the babies. An owner would swear that the child was his daughter or his niece and ward; and to support this he would present a swarm of perjured witnesses bought at the union range for Chinese testimony -- $5 for a safe job, a little more for a dangerous one."

These changes impacted the Methodist Mission. Otis and Eliza Gibson were aging, and Otis was frequently ill. The WHMS decided that their mission needed a more concerted rescue strategy. Chairperson Mrs. Laura P. Williams reported, "The time has come to adopt other and more aggressive modes of work."

The Dangerous World of Rescues

Meanwhile public opinion was shifting to sympathy for the enslaved girls. The public may have been prejudiced against Chinese men whom they believed were taking jobs from white men. But citizens disliked the idea of slavery even more, and over time public opinion shifted and more people sympathized with the girls and young women. The press paid attention and began to publish articles scorning the slave trade and demanding action from Congress.

Yet in Chinatown the brothels sprouted like poisonous mushrooms. Although slavery was illegal in the United States, prostitution was not. Every brothel owner swore that the girls either worked by choice or were serving an indentured period to pay off their ship passage. It was all perfectly legal. If rescuers asked the women if they wanted to be rescued the answer was often "No." Sometimes they were too afraid to ask for rescue – afraid of their owners, or the Tongs, or even of the Mission since they were told that the Mission women simply resold them into even worse circumstances. Many of them were too far gone in mental illness or opium addiction. And even if a girl escaped on her own she was marked by the distinctive costume most of the Chinese prostitutes wore: black silk pajamas with embroidered flowers. The costumes were dead giveaways of an escaped prostitute. If she approached a policeman he may be a Tong informant and immediately return her to the brothel, or she would be pursued by Tongs members eager to reclaim their property.

California citizens began a petition drive to send to President McKinley regarding Chinese slavery in the state. *The Call* wrote that the petition drive seems "to have filled a 'long felt want' in missionary circles and to have met with a responsive chord in the minds of the people generally." The petition was a hot topic in the city of San Francisco and several ministers openly discussed it from their Sunday pulpits and encouraged their congregations to sign it. Petition workers also brought it to a ministers' meeting and to the public in their effort to garner thousands of signatures.

Rev. Frederic Masters complimented the press on their work to stop the slave trade. "To the honor of the San Francisco press be it said, their defense of these helpless girls and their motherly rescuers was most manly. Their exposé of slavery was fearless."

As the number of rescues and court placements of the girls swelled, the Missions were bursting at the seams. And with a steady increase of young children among the rescued, both Missions looked to establishing orphanages and schools for the little ones. By 1892 there were 1500 hundred native born Chinese children in San Francisco, and these numbers were growing rapidly. An MEC Missions Report said:

"It is evident that the increasing demand for evangelistic work among the Chinese necessitates enlarged facilities for aggressive measures, which our present quarters, located on the line that divides Chinatown from the white population, does not afford. We must have a place right in the slums of the Chinese district, where heroic street work is even now going on. Such a place is very difficult to secure, as rents are high, and the prejudice against such a movement is strong and shared by the property holders, who do not hesitate to rent their property for the liquor traffic, but refuse to do so for religious services. The sum of $500, appropriated by the Missionary Society, is utterly inadequate to meet this case. We should have at least $1,000 per annum with which to inaugurate and sustain such an enterprise."

The Story of Lilac Chen

Lilac Chen's experience illustrates these later developments. As a girl, Lilac Chen was smuggled from China and sold to a large brothel in San Francisco. She was eventually sold and resold as a house servant, which at first was an improvement but the improvement did not last. She later wrote:

"Everywhere I had been they were very kind to me except this last place. . . . Oh, this woman was so awful! They say she was a domestic servant before and was cruelly treated. She used to make me carry a big fat baby on my back and make me wash his diapers. And you know, to wash you have to stoop over, and then he pulls you back, and cry and cry. Oh, I got desperate, I didn't care what happened to me, I just pinched his cheek. . . . She, his mother, went and burned a red hot iron tong and burnt me on the arm."

Lilac did not know Christ, but Christ knew her. He put the rescue in motion. A white woman crossed paths with the girl and spotted the burn on Lilac's arm. The woman reported Lilac's case to the Presbyterian Mission Home. The woman described Lilac as best she could but had not seen the girl clearly. When the Presbyterian rescuers arrived at the house where Lilac worked they had an inaccurate description and could not find her among the other servants. Lilac later wrote:

"They described me much bigger than I was so when they came they didn't recognize me. And then the woman who reported to the mission said, 'Why didn't you take her? She's the girl,' and then they came back again. But even then, they weren't sure that I was the one, so they undressed me and examined my body and found where the woman had beaten me black and blue all over. And then they took me to the home. Oh, it was in the pouring rain! I was scared to death. You know, change from change, and all strangers, and I didn't know where I was going. Away from my own people and in the pouring rain. And they took me, a fat policeman carried me all the way from Jackson Street, where I was staying, to Sacramento Street to the mission. So I got my freedom there."

Some girls risked everything to get to the Mission on their own. In 1897 two young servants, 12-year-old Suey Leen and Dong Ho, were living in terrible conditions. They heard about the "Jesus women" and decided to escape to the Presbyterian mission. The girls did not think they could escape together so they decided that Dong Ho must go first and then come back for Suey Leen. Dong Ho escaped with her life and a handkerchief containing her worldly possessions, which the Mission recorded: "Two broken Chinese toys, a pair of worn-out chopsticks, a cracked bowl and two soiled garments."

Dong Ho was desperate for them to rescue Suey Leen. But the girl's mistress had moved the child after Dong Ho's disappearance, and the missionaries could not find her. They prayed for the missing child and waited for news.

Three months later a dirty, starving and exhausted young girl showed up at the Mission door. She did not give her name when the women brought her in. Dong Ho appeared on the staircase and when she saw the girl she ran to her and threw her arms around her. Donaldina Cameron later wrote, "I never saw anything so affecting as when they saw one another. I thought that they would be broken in two with their hugs. Then we realized that it was Suey Leen. And since then they have always been inseparable."

Thomas Filbin

Rescue work was not limited to the Mission women. The Rev. Thomas Filben ministered in an MEC church in Sacramento. The city had an active Chinese slave trade of its own where girls who were brought into San Francisco were sold to the inland city and the brothels close by its large gambling dens. Rev. Filben and his church helped to rescue many of these girls and sent them back to San Francisco and the safety of the Methodist Mission.

Thomas had gotten word that a girl needed rescue from one Chin Ah Fee, a notorious slave owner and highbinder. The rescue was successful, and the girl and Thomas left on the local train for San Francisco. But the girl was valuable, and Chin Ah Fee had no intention of letting her go. Several American constables were in his pay and the Chinese man lost no time telegraphing one of the men on his payroll, Constable Kincaid at Davisville. The train would be passing through Davisville Station where Kincaid was supposed to arrest the woman and hold her until Chin Ah Fee could arrive to reclaim his fleeing property.

Kincaid roused several local highbinders to come with him, and when the train stopped in Davisville, Pastor Filben looked out the window to see a group of armed highbinders with a tall white policeman standing in the middle of the group. Kincaid saw Thomas and the woman through the train window and shouted at them to come out. Thomas yelled back that they would not be setting foot off this train and that the constable had no right to arrest her. The conductors did not allow the constable on board because they did not like the look of the men who were with him. The train pulled out of the station. But Kinkaid was determined to earn his bribe and telegraphed another constable located farther down the line near the Elmira station. He said that the constable was to board the train and arrest the woman without fail.

At the Elmira stop this constable got on board and spotted Thomas and the woman. He demanded that Thomas turn the frightened girl over to him. He refused. "You cannot have her. Show me your warrant." There was no warrant, but the constable showed the telegram he had received from Kincaid. Thomas said that was not good enough and that if he laid a hand on the woman he would answer for it. Things might have turned violent except for the other passengers. They were in sympathy with the clergyman and the terrified woman, and sided with Thomas against the constable. Amid cries of "Show us the warrant!" the officer beat a hasty retreat off the train.

Thomas believed that more telegraphs had gone out and at least one of them would have gone to a Tong headquarters in San Francisco. The San Francisco train station had a large police presence and was unlikely to be dangerous, but the two had to take a ferry over the Bay to reach the Mission. Highbinder gangs were likely to be waiting at the less secure ferry gates for the two as they walked out to the hired carriages. Instead of leaving the ferry house and the gates to walk to the waiting carriages, Thomas arranged with a driver to pick them up right outside the doors of the station. This he did, and once his passengers were inside the carriage the driver drove out a side entrance and made for the Mission.

The highbinders quickly realized what had happened and pursued the carriage right up to the Mission gates. Thomas jumped out and pulled the woman with him, shouting for help as he did so. The Tong gang members tried to pull the woman away and into a waiting carriage, but Mission staff members poured out the door to help. The girl's clothes were torn, and she lost her shoes in the struggle but at last Thomas, the girl, and the mission staff were safely behind the sturdy doors of the mission where the highbinders dared not follow. The Sacramento newspapers had a field day reporting on the rescue.

The Story of Tye Leung

Tye Leung was born in San Francisco in 1887. In crowded Chinatown, large families lived together in small apartments. Leung's parents, their eight children, and an aunt and uncle lived packed tightly together in two rooms. Tye Leung badly wanted an education and to be a teacher but the local school that served the Chinese and Japanese children only went through sixth grade. Asian children were not allowed to attend public schools with white children.

Her brothers and sisters did not go past the 6th grade and her family could see no reason why Leung should be an exception. They had already arranged a marriage for Leung's older sister. The sister was only 14 years old and her would-be bridegroom was a 40-year-old man living in Montana. The man had already paid the parents for the bride, but the sister ran away from home and married a teenage boy instead. (Small blame to her.)

Rather than return the money, the parents decided to substitute twelve-year-old Tye Leung. Leung ran as quickly as her sister had, but instead of marrying a young man she fled to the Presbyterian Mission for shelter and an education. The women took her in and refused to release her to her parents, who had to abandon the plan to send her to Montana and an unwanted marriage.

At the Presbyterian Home Leung learned English and made friends with one of the teachers. Tye Leung later wrote, "The teacher, who was Miss Wesley, later Mrs. Cook, was very fond of me. She took a liking to me and got me clothes, bathed me, took me to different church meetings, and showed me off."

Donaldina Cameron also took to the bright, brave girl. Tye Leung blossomed at the Mission and as she grew older became Donaldina's aide and interpreter. She even went with Donaldina on rescues and helped her with court matters. Tye Leung would later become famous as the first Chinese woman in the country to legally vote for the President of the United States. "Celestial Maid cast her vote" trumpeted the approving *San Francisco Call*.

She remained generally popular in Chinatown and in the press even when she married a white man, Charles Frederick Schulze. Like Ida Hull before her, the couple had to travel out of state to marry. "Little Dan Cupid does strange tricks" reported one newspaper.

Donaldina and the Great Work

"We stand at the outset face to face with the great American idea of opening this free and broad land as a refuge and a shelter to all who would seek its shores. We have stood within our magnificent domain, and feeling that we had room enough for all, and that we possessed the happiest and freest form of government of any nation on earth, we have said in the hearing of all the families of men, 'Lift up your heads, oh ye gates, and be ye lifted up ye asylum doors, that whosoever will may enter in!'"
(Congregationalist minister D.A.L. Stone)

One of the Presbyterians' fiercest missionaries and rescuers was an immigrant to the United States herself, Miss Donaldina Cameron. The highbinders called her *Fahn Quai* -- the "white devil." She bore it like a badge of honor.

Donaldina was born on a New Zealand sheep ranch, the youngest of seven children. The family immigrated to the United States in 1871 when she was only 2 years old. When she was 19 she was engaged for a short time to a young man named Fred Young but felt a strong call to be a missionary. Her fiancé had no interest whatsoever in serving as a missionary, so the couple broke their engagement.

However, Donaldina had no idea where she was supposed to serve. She prayed and talked to friends, and soon Mrs. Mary Ann Brown heard of Donaldina's uncertainty. Mary Ann was the president of the Presbyterian's Occidental Women's Board of Foreign Missions and suggested to Donaldina that she go to work at the San Francisco Mission for a year. The young woman could teach sewing to the girls and help Margaret Culbertson in whatever way she could.

Donaldina agreed to work there for a year. She stayed for thirty.

Her first year consisted of teaching sewing and helping an aging Margaret. At first "helping" meant aiding with paperwork. Donaldina did that work dutifully but what she loved was rescue missions. She was a woman after Margaret's own heart. Not only was Donaldina fearless, she also had a knack for locating false walls and trapdoors. She would point out the false fronts to the policemen who accompanied her. They wielded sledgehammers and axes to knock down locked doors and hastily erected hiding places, and to take out the women hidden inside.

Margaret Culbertson then taught her how to work the court system, writing the letters of guardianship that kept rescued girls from being reclaimed by their owners.

Donaldina had found her calling, but before long she realized that God had called her to far more then she bargained for. Only two years after Donaldina arrived, Margaret died from injuries inflicted by a terrified young woman. The Board thought that Donaldina showed great promise as a leader, but she was too young and too new at the work to be appointed Superintendent of the Mission Home.

Mary H. Field took over for Margaret and Donaldina stayed as a teacher for the next three years. Then Mary resigned, and the Board was faced with a choice: appoint an older and more experienced woman to the post, or appoint 30-year-old Donaldina instead. Her age worked against her, but her talent and drive were unmistakable. She received the appointment.

Will Irwin wrote about these early days. "The managers of the mission were doubtful about her capacity; the white watchmen of the Chinese, who were becoming a little anxious over the frequency of the rescues, laughed in their sleeves. Within the year, these watchmen were being discharged because of the great number of girls lost to their employers. Miss Cameron's campaign was aggressive from the first. Where the other workers had depended upon a police force not above suspicion of graft, and always half-hearted, she depended upon herself. Knowing that the legal problem could be solved in time and that the slave business, being strictly a business, could not stand uncertainty, she made rescue work her first concern. She became lawyer, detective, and above all, raider."

In the face of active rescue attempts, The Tongs had made it much harder for the prostitutes to escape the brothels on their own. The Presbyterian Home was willing to rescue the girls who wanted out, but the girls had to get messages to the Mission to come. The Home put up posters all over Chinatown with contact information written in Cantonese and English. The Tongs tore them down, but the Home put them right back up again. The Home also paid delivery men to smuggle messages into the brothels when they delivered food and drink. Mission workers contacted many girls by doing social work at the brothels. The madams had no right to keep out legal visitations and many a message passed hands this way.

Sometimes brothel visitors themselves would bring word to the Mission that a girl wanted rescue. The Exclusion Act kept unmarried Chinese women from legally entering this country, and young men were desperate to find a wife of their own. If a visitor found a prostitute that he liked he was more than willing to marry her. In most cases the girl's owners were perfectly willing to sell her, but the cost of her lost wages was very high. These Chinese laborers did not have the hundreds or thousands of dollars demanded. They often came to the Home for help.

Before agreeing, Donaldina would smuggle in a message to the girl to see if she wanted to be rescued. She almost always did, for being married even to a poor man was vastly preferable to a short and unhappy life in a brothel. If the rescue went well, then Donaldina would take her back to the Home to live for a year so that the workers could be certain that the girl learned a good trade and that her young man was serious about marrying her. The hopeful groom paid a small but steady sum for the girl's room and board.

A Tong Member Finds Romance

In an account told in Carol Green Wilson's *Chinatown Quest*, one Tong member had met and fallen in love with a slave girl working a brothel on May Fong Alley. This was not uncommon in San Francisco where many men wanted a wife but only prostitutes were available. The slaveowners were usually willing to sell a girl but she was expensive: working prostitutes made their owners a thousand dollars a year for several years. Few working men could afford such a ransom, and many worked for years so so they could ransom the girl they wanted to marry.

Making matters worse for our Tong member, the girl was owned by a rival Tong who would be sure to charge him more. The young man could not afford to ransom her, and the girl had decided to kill herself instead of working any longer in the brothel. He assured her that if she ran away he would take care of her.

They made their plans. She managed her escape from the brothel and fled to the lodging house on Dupont Street where her lover lived. But the brothel guards had witnessed her escape and pelted after her. The guards burst into the house just behind her and kept her and her lover prisoner until the slaveowner arrived.

Upon finding out that the man belonged to a rival Tong, they decided not to kill him as that would have started a Tong war. However, they had every right to demand a large sum of money for her right then and there -- $1000, in the late 1800s an impossible sum to raise quickly. When the young man could not pay, the Tong members swept the girl away. Her young man was frantic. As a Tong highbinder he knew exactly where the Tongs' number one enemy lived -- at the Presbyterian Mission. Swallowing his pride, he shoved his way through the crowded streets as soon as he could and arrived at the Mission's front porch. In broken English he begged Donaldina to come and rescue the girl. Donaldina motioned to the Home's interpreter, petite Kum Ching. "Take off your apron quickly," Donaldina said. "We must go on another rescue."

Usually Donaldina would have sent to police headquarters for an escort but there was no time. By God's grace they spotted a policeman standing on a street corner. He was an older, heavy man and puffed when he walked, but he came at their call. The young man guided them through the dark streets to the rival Tong's headquarter in Ross Alley, sure that the girl was being held there while they decided what to do with her. Once there the young man stayed out of sight lest his presence start a Tong war. Donaldina, Ching and the policeman would have to handle the rescue themselves.

It was nighttime and only one Tong member stood guard at the front door. Elderly and half-asleep, he did not react when petite Kum Ching dashed up the steep stairs to the second story porch, ran past him, and flung open the unlocked door. Donaldina was right behind her. The gatekeeper immediately recognized *Fahn Quai*, the White Devil, and flung himself towards the door to slam it shut. Kim Ching struggled to keep the door open. "Hurry!" she shouted to the massive policeman, who lumbered as fast as he could up the steps. He shouted at the gatekeeper to stand down.

Donaldina heard a girl scream. She pushed past the gatekeeper and ran down the hallway, made a right turn, and was just in time to see a heavy wooden door slammed in her face. The screams were abruptly cut off. The policeman had sufficiently cowed the gatekeeper and joined Donaldina at the heavy interior door. He tried to open it, but it was too thick even for him and he had to go for help.

Donaldina and Kum Ching were frantic as the screams were replaced by the sound of dragging furniture and banging.

Were they killing the girl right there in the room? It took 20 minutes for the policeman to return with two more men and sledgehammers, and just then the room went quiet. The policeman battered in the door and burst inside, the women behind them – only to see a calm and unruffled group of men holding a meeting. Thirteen Chinese Tong members sat around a table smoking water pipes and looking quizzically at their visitors.

The policemen, Donaldina and Kum Ching searched the room but could find nothing. Even Donaldina, who had a near-supernatural talent for finding false doors and hidden rooms, could find nothing. Frustrated and worried, she stepped out onto the fire escape for a breath of fresh air.

By now it was early morning and the city was dimly lit in gray light. Across the alley a building painter was already perched on a scaffold. He spotted Donaldina on the fire escape and called out to her, "They took her up through the skylight, across the roof next door!"

Donaldina sprang back into action. She murmured to the fittest of the policemen to follow her. Together they scrambled down the steep outside stairs of the Tong headquarters, hurried down the sidewalk and took the flight of stairs leading up to the neighboring house's porch. They scaled another flight of stairs to the second building's porch. They knocked heavily on the door and the policeman loudly announced their presence.

A Chinese man opened the door. When they told him that they were seeking a kidnapped girl he protested that he ran a good Christian home and that the only young woman here was his daughter. Donaldina and the policeman came in and searched anyway. They did not see or hear a woman but Donaldina spotted an open skylight and a ladder in the room. There was a wooden wardrobe on the room whose door opened slightly.

"Mission Home," Donaldina said loudly -- and a terrified girl climbed out of the wardrobe and ran into Donaldina's arms. Escorted by the policemen, the two women left the house. The girl was weak and trembling as they made their slow way down the steep stairs.

Meanwhile the Tong guards had been roused by the commotion and were gathering inside the headquarters. Kum Ching understood their whispered Cantonese and told the two policemen with her that they had better leave the house for the public street. They did but a dozen Tong members followed on their heels. Donaldina, the third policeman and the fainting girl reached the street at the same time as her friends and the Tong members. The policemen were badly outnumbered, and the situation looked grim.

Then something happened. Like the painter who had come to work very early, a tour group of Americans had gotten an early start on their walking trip to Chinatown. The group was passing by the Tong headquarters just at this tense moment. The guide knew about the Christian Missions and their rescues and he recognized Donaldina. He stopped the group and explained what was happening just as Donaldina handed the girl over to Kum Ching. The interpreter comforted the girl in her native Cantonese. The tour group broke into spontaneous applause and the Tong members turned around and quickly disappeared into their headquarters, shutting the door behind them.

Were the painter and the tour group mere coincidences? No. They were miracles.

Once Donaldina had confirmed a girl's name and location she enlisted the help of the local police or a men's volunteer organization. She set spies to watch the brothel to make sure the girl was not moved to prevent a rescue. On the rescue date the group quietly gathered after midnight a few blocks from the targeted brothel. The men would tote along axes and sledgehammers for breaking down doors and most of the women armed themselves with hatchets in case of a fight.

San Francisco's streets were lit with gas lamps, but Chinatown was in darkness. This was an advantage to criminals, but it was also an advantage to the rescue party, who quietly made their way down the darkened streets. The party paused outside the mouth of the street or alley that the brothel faced. There were sometimes loiterers or customers outside the brothel, but when they caught sight of the burly policemen they melted away into the darkness.

Some of the brothels were street level and some were located on the upper stories of rickety buildings. Donaldina and her party would carefully climb up the fire escapes or shallow porches to the barred and locked front door. The men raised their sledgehammers and with a few strong blows the door shuddered and burst open.

The men went in first to hold off any attackers while

Donaldina and the other women rushed down the narrow hallway and tore open the curtains that veiled the tiny cell-like rooms. As they went they would shout the name of the girl who had asked for rescue. When she answered the party brought her out. They never rescued a girl who did not ask to be rescued, but if another girl said she wanted to come too they would take her. If the rescue party found small children or babies, they would take them without question and wait for the courts to sort it out.

Sometimes the madams had heard the sledgehammer blows and quickly hid the girls below trap doors or behind false walls. But Donaldina had a nose like a bloodhound when it came to sniffing out the hiding places. She would point them out and the men used their axes with a good will.

By then all hell was breaking loose as the sledgehammer blows and the screams of the furious madams woke up the neighbors up and down the alley. The rescue party grabbed up the rescued girls and children and left quickly with the policeman forming a cordon around them. The men escorted them safely to the Mission and Donaldina firmly closed and locked the doors against any assault. The Tongs hardly appreciated Donaldina's activities: they built an effigy of her and plunged a knife into its heart. With great aplomb, Donaldina ignored it.

Arnold Genthe was a writer who knew Donaldina well. In his book *As I Remember* he wrote:

"A challenging member of the [Presbyterian] community was Donaldina Cameron, for many

years the head of the Chinese Presbyterian Mission, and a truly noble and courageous woman. At the risk of her life, which was often threatened, she had rescued many girls from the toils of the slave-traffic. Among the Chinese, daughters were not looked upon with favor except as potential concubines to be sold for a price, or as possible bearers of sons. It was not unusual for them to be sold into slavery between the ages of four and ten, to be resold by their owners when they were fourteen, either as concubines or sing-song girls.

"I got to know Miss Cameron quite well, and she let me come to the Mission to take pictures of her protégées -- lovely little creatures poetically named Tea Rose, Apple Blossom, Plum Blossom. Miss Cameron was not a tight-lipped reformer who wished to make the world over into a monotone. She had respect and admiration for the art and literature of China and she saw that the girls she had taken under her wing were educated in its tradition."

As Donaldina's fame grew, her home country of New Zealand was inordinately proud of her. In May 1915, New Zealand's *Fielding Star* reported on an article about her in an American magazine. The profile was entitled "Donaldina Cameron, White Devil." *Fielding Star* reported:

"The *American Magazine* runs a regular section under the title, 'Interesting People.' In the April section appears a page devoted to 'The White Devil.' This is the name given by the Chinese of San

Francisco to Miss Donaldina Cameron, of whom it is written: 'No other person on all the Pacific Coast is so hated by the Chinese highbinders. She has rescued from slavery not less than 1500 Chinese girls in the 20 years she has had charge of the rescue work of the Occidental Board of Foreign Missions in San Francisco. Miss Cameron has gone at midnight into the farthest corners of those rookeries that were the Chinatown of old San Francisco, has chopped down doors, crawled through secret passages reached by panels opening with hidden springs, and found her quarry, bound and held at point of pistol. She has raided Chinese gambling dens where girls sat in the centre of the table rolling cigarettes for the gamblers, and made wild night rides across unknown country with the rescued girls. She has snatched them from their keepers on the street and made away with them through shrieking mobs of Chinese. She has risked her life in a hundred ways to rescue young girls from lives of wretchedness and crime. And Miss Cameron was born in New Zealand."

Will Irwin reported on one of those rescues.

"Once Miss Cameron followed a five-year-old slave to a Chinese camp in the foot-hills of the Sierras. She drove ten miles by night with one Healey, a country constable. They hitched their horse outside the gambling-house where the girl was known to be, and peeped through a hole in the screen which shielded the door. The child was sitting on a table, rolling cigarettes for six gamblers, who were playing fan-tan. Overthrowing the screen and rushing on the little girl, Miss Cameron snatched her up, and Healey held back the gamblers at the point of his revolver. As they backed through the door, a Chinese seemed to rise out of the ground. He drew a revolver and fired point-blank at Miss Cameron. The Chinese slowness with a gun, traditional in the west, saved her, for Healey had time to strike it up, so that the bullet splintered the ceiling. They drove ten miles to civilization, and all the way Healey kept his revolver in hand against pursuit and attack."

As Donaldina grew older she began leaving the rescues to the younger women. She stayed very active in the court system and running the Presbyterian Home, and in founding additional ministries to the Chinese in California. Over the course of her work the Presbyterian mission rescued more than 3000 children and young women from hideous lives and lonely deaths.

The Devil Came Down to Chinatown

Battle in the Courts

"One of the worst features of this secret society--and the same applies to all the other highbinder associations-- is its mischievous interference with the administration of justice. With unlimited funds at their disposal to employ counsel, suborn perjury, bribe the venal, and employ agents to intimidate the other side, it is almost impossible to secure the conviction of the criminal around whom this unscrupulous society has thrown its protecting arms." (Rev. Frederic Masters)

Rescue efforts did not end with physically removing the woman or child from the brothel or home where she was imprisoned. The Tongs had become more sophisticated as it became harder to bring in women through American ports and as the Christian missions became more and more successful at their rescue work. Prostitutes were rich sources of income for their owners and for the owners' lawyers, guards and investors. So the Tongs, with the help of their white lawyers, turned to the courts.

In his book *Among the Highbinders* Rev. Frederic Masters wrote about the Tongs' role in the courts.

"When a slave woman escapes from a house of ill fame in which a highbinder society is interested, it is a common thing to swear out some charge against her, such as grand larceny. She is arrested, thrown into prison, and bailed out by her owners, who then have her in their power. If she agrees to return to the bagnio [brothel] the complainant fails to identify her, and the case is dismissed. When the woman escapes to the mission and is arrested, the missionaries are able to protect the poor woman from the villains who, by means of the processes of law, would drag her back again to a den of infamy.

"In some cases the Chinaman who has helped the woman to escape is discovered, and is summarily dealt with unless reparation is speedily made. In two cases that have come under the writer's notice these men have been charged with murder and thrown into prison. But for the interference of the writer they would, in all probability, have lost their lives or been sentenced to penal servitude."

As more rescues were followed by more court cases, the missions learned to fight fire with fire. Immediately following a rescue, the missions pressed for guardianship rights for the children and teens in their care. The courts were usually sympathetic to the mission guardianship requests, but the Tong lawyers just as quickly brought civil and criminal charges against the missions.

The writ of habeas corpus was a popular legal weapon. The writs applied to cases where a person was kept in custodial care against their will. Upon receiving the writ, the custodian was required to produce the person in a court of law to review their custodial rights. If the court determined that the person was being unlawfully detained, the person was immediately released.

The writs were meant to be weapons against kidnapping or forced custodial arrangements. But the Tongs' lawyers used them to compel girls and young women to return to the brothels by claiming that the missions where the girls had taken refuge were keeping them against their will.

Mission workers would have to bring the girls to court to hear arguments from the Tongs' lawyers. The attorneys would argue that a slaveowner was a child's parent, or a girl's husband. This was usually an outright lie but many times the girls were terrified of the owners and refused to testify on their own behalf. However, lacking their testimony that they had been enslaved, the court would release them. Their owners took immediate possession.

The Missions had lawyers as well, most of them volunteering their services. Several retired judges also supported the mission work and provided invaluable advice and relationships in the San Francisco legal community. Sometimes the Six Companies, Chinatown's legitimate business authority, stepped in to support the Missions if the plaintiff was a particularly unsavory individual.

In 1895 the Methodist mission had rescued a 7-year-old little girl named Ah Soo. A Chinese man calling himself Charley Hung claimed that the mission had imprisoned his daughter, and applied for a writ of habeas corpus to compel her to appear in court. The Chinese consul and the Six Companies often stayed out of these cases or even spoke for the plaintiff. But Charley Hung was a notorious convict, slaveowner and opium dealer and had embarrassed the Six Companies who witnessed for the mission. Hung failed to gain custody of little Ah Soo.

In another case the federal authorities ended up on the side of the angels. Donaldina Cameron and her rescue party took an enslaved child named Ah Fah from owner Tong Dock. The owner vehemently protested the child's removal and followed the rescue party with its police escort to the police station. There he convinced the police that he was the child's father and that they should keep the girl overnight in jail rather than release her to the Presbyterian Mission.

He planned to return early the next morning with a writ of habeas corpus, prove that the police were keeping the child unlawfully as she had committed no crime, and take immediate possession of her.

The ploy worked, and the local police released the child to her owner. However, Donaldina had not been idle either. She had alerted the federal authorities that the local police might be a shade too lenient with Tong Duck. When the man pulled Ah Fah out of the police station, the federal authorities arrested him on a charge of involuntary servitude and remanded the child to the Mission's care.

Some of the rescued slaves did fight back in court. In 1902, Margarita Lake of the Methodist Mission rescued a 10-year-old named Chen Ha Wau from a merchant's home where she worked as a *mui tsai*, an indentured servant. The merchant Fong Quong was furious at losing his unpaid servant and her future sale, and claimed that the little girl was his daughter. He filed a writ of habeas corpus compelling the girl to appear in court. The missionaries accompanied Wau to court and stood ready to do battle. Fong Quong brought his wife and they together stated that they were the child's parents and that Margarita Lake had kidnapped her.

But young Wau was having none of it. She bravely testified that she was born in China and that her mother had sold her to slavers. When she arrived in San Francisco she was sold to the merchant and his wife to serve as a slave in his household. Judge Frank J. Murasky asked her where she wanted to live. She pointed to Fong Quong's wife then said loudly, "I want to go to the mission because she is not my mother and I want to go to school." The judge ruled in her favor.

Some of the girls went even further in pursuit of an education and a new life. A Chinese Gold Rush miner came to the United States and brought his pregnant wife, a teenage girl, and a toddler daughter with him. They left an older daughter behind. Once they arrived in the country, the baby was born on U.S. soil. Within a few years the mother died, and the teenager married. The father returned to China and left his baby daughter in the care of her married sister. When the little girl turned 13, her father returned to the U.S. to take her back to China to be married, although she had never set foot in the country.

But this girl was determined to stay in the United States and to receive an American education. The father insisted that he would let the girl go to school in China, but she did not believe him. She later wrote:

> "One of my older sisters had been married in China, against her will, after she had been just a very short time in school. I felt that if I went back with him I would very shortly be married, and that I

would not have anything to say about it. My father brought me to San Francisco, and bought my ticket to China. The night before the boat sailed, I told him I would go to the Mission and throw myself on their protection. I was resolved not to marry, to have an education instead. If I once consented to go to China, I would be lost. There would be no police, one could not telephone for help, the American consul could not help me."

She escaped from her father and found her way to the Presbyterian Mission Home and appealed for help to Donaldina Cameron. Since the girl had been born on U.S. soil, Cameron took her to see a judge. The judge ruled that she could not be forced to leave the country to go to China and she could stay at the Mission. She would eventually go on to graduate from college.

The Story of Woon T'Sun

Tragically, even biological parents sometimes sold their girls to the highest bidder. Their experience in China had taught them to treat girl children as an economic burden, and to make whatever bargain they could. Judge Reardon commented in a child custody case, "In these Chinese cases of maternity claimed, there always lurks a suspicion that the claim is made because, according to Mongolian methods, the child is valuable property. Yet a few years and this infant will, as prices in the slave market rule, be worth from fifteen hundred to two thousand dollars; and it might well be that the grief, real or simulated, of the mother has a money basis."

Six-year-old Woon T'Sun was the only surviving child of her widowed father but that did not endear her to him. The father had borrowed a good amount of money from the infamous Kum Mah, a Chinese madam who ran several brothels and had a nice side business in loan sharking. The father could not pay back a loan, so Kum Mah generously offered to forgive his debt in exchange for his young daughter. The father agreed, left his little girl with the notorious madam, and sailed back to China. The child was worth $1000 in the slave market even then, and if she lived until her teenage years she would be worth twice that.

In those days Miss Emma Cable worked under Margaret Culbertson of the Presbyterian Mission. Emma did house-to-house visitations as a missionary and social worker. She helped to get food and medical help for the prostitutes, and was in an excellent position to identify women and children for rescue.

One day she visited a brothel in Bartlett Alley owned by Kum Mah and discovered little Woon T'Sun living there. Emma arranged for a rescue team but before they could get there, the child disappeared. Emma and Margaret Culbertson kept searching for her. A few months later that they discovered that she was with her owner Kim Mah in a building on Dupont Street. Kum Mah used the child to run errands to various brothels and gambling dens in Chinatown. The Mission women got word to Detective Cox of the situation and on November 16, 1890 he arrested the little girl as she was coming out of a brothel. He delivered the child to Margaret, who wasted no time in taking out letters of guardianship.

But Kum Mah had not made her illegal fortune by sitting

on the sidelines, and she and her American lawyers immediately filed a writ of habeas corpus to force Margaret and Woon T'Sun into the courtroom. The woman had the Tongs' help since the gangs did not want to establish a precedent for the Mission rescuing children from under their collective noses. Prominent Tong members advised Kum Mah and donated to her legal fund.

The Tong's lawyers agreed that Kim Mah should not serve as the child's guardian, so they suggested a woman named May Sing instead. But the Mission's lawyers pointed out that Kim Mah had raised May Sing and had put her to work as a prostitute, and eventually put her in charge of one of the brothels. This was the path she had planned for little Woon T'Sun as well.

The court case was a sensation in San Francisco. The entire Occidental Board showed up in court nearly every day, and the presence of these distinguished ladies kept the public's attention riveted on the court case. One of the Board members later wrote that Kum Mah's white American lawyers deliberately made the courtroom unpleasant for the ladies, hoping to keep them from attending court. She reported, "A lawyer asked Miss Culbertson indecent and insulting questions -- insinuating that they were not fit to have the care of a child, and that they sold children back to slavery for money, and took bribes for letting them go, and other absurd charges."

But the ladies were determined to stay. "This plan will not work now; we are determined to see this matter through and find out whether these little girls can be protected by the courts of California." The Board stayed. Along with Margaret

Culbertson the women attended court over 20 times during the next several weeks.

The case grew so scandalous that even the national press got into the action. Journalists from New York and Chicago told the story of Margaret Culbertson, the brave Board ladies, and little Woon T'Soon who was in constant terror that the judge would turn her back over to her owner.

In the end all was well: the judge ruled in favor of Margaret's guardianship. The public breathed a collective sigh of relief, the Mission Board and workers went on their knees to thank God, and Woon T'Sun grew up happy and healthy in the care of the Presbyterian Mission.

The Devil Came Down to Chinatown

Margarita Lake

In 1902 Margarita Lake rescued ten-year-old Chen Ha Wau. Although a Chinese merchant claimed the child was his daughter, Lake feared the girl was a "slave" purchased to perform domestic service for the merchant's family…. When Judge Frank J. Murasky asked her where she wanted to go, she said, "'I want to go to the mission because she,' pointing to the merchant's wife, 'is not my mother and I want to go to school.'" The judge granted custody to the Methodist mission. (Wendy Rouse Jorae, The Children of Chinatown)

Margarita Lake never planned to be a missionary. She studied to be a classical pianist and looked forward to traveling to Germany for further study. Then she attended a Salvation Army camp meeting, received Christ, and shortly thereafter heard God's call to missionary work.

In the fall of 1894 she enrolled at the Lucy Rider Meyer Deaconess Training School in Chicago and was ordained a deaconess two years later. She had a strong desire to work with the Chinese and assumed that meant she was to travel as a foreign missionary to China. But problem after problem kept her from going there. God's hand in these circumstances became clear when she encountered the WHMS Oriental Bureau, who hired Margarita and her mother Kate in 1896 to work as staff members and missionaries at the Methodist Home. Margarita was 23 years old.

Mother and daughter worked in the WHMS in San Francisco until 1903, and in 1910 Margarita married Ernest Garton. After her husband's death, Margarita returned to California where she was instrumental in helping found the Chinese Baptist Church of San Mateo, California.

Margarita was known for her courage in rescues and for her shrewdness dealing with the courts. One day at the Methodist Mission she received a note from a girl named Ah Oye who was desperate for rescue. Ah Oye wrote, "I am take time write few lines to you today. I am want you come here. Bring me to city you there school all time. My name Ah Oye. My house be green and red. You must be sure and come here. If you no come here I be sure and die. My mama scold me and want sell me to the bad place."

Margarita noted the postal mark and began trying to find the house in a sea of green and red Chinatown houses. A second letter soon arrived. Ah Oye wrote that the problem was her stepmother who beat her and threatened to sell her. Margarita searched for the girl, but we do not know if she found her. She had many letters of this type; sometimes they found the girls and sometimes not. They always tried.

Some Mission workers and visitors were so taken with a child that they took matters into their own hands. Miss Anna Jones traveled to San Francisco in 1897 to attend a Christian convention. While there she visited the Methodist Mission and met Margarita, then the Director of the Home. She met several of the children living there including a terrified young girl who was about to be deported to China. In some kidnapping cases, deportation was a blessing if the child or woman had family waiting for them at the Hong Kong dock. But many of the victims had no way of reaching their families, or their families had sold them in the first place. When these girls were deported they were let off the ship in Hong Kong with no money and no family.

This young girl faced this situation. She had no idea where her family lived in China and was terrified of leaving this country. The Mission wanted to keep her here and argued her case with officials but made no headway. Anna was so upset at the thought of the desperate girl being sent back to China that she went to the Customs Collector to plead against the child's deportation. She even offered to adopt the girl and raise her to keep her in this country. But the man would not be moved; the child was here illegally and back to China she must go.

Anna rushed back to the Home to get advice from Margarita, but the Director was not there. So, Anna did the only thing she could think of to save the child: she took the girl with her and fled to Las Vegas where she raised the little girl as her own daughter. Legally it was a kidnapping. In God's eyes it was a rescue.

Like Donaldina Cameron, Margarita frequently went on raids to rescue prostitutes and their children. One of the ways she enabled the girls to contact her was by acting as a licensed social investigator for the city of San Francisco. This position allowed her to enter brothels during the day to investigate conditions. If a prostitute asked for her help when she was there, so much the better.

One time Margarita got word that a little boy was living in

terrible conditions in a brothel on Washington Street. As a social investigator she could make her way inside the brothel and bring the child out to the Methodist Home. They were not taking in boys, but he was covered in vermin, so she undressed the toddler to give him a bath -- and discovered that the little "boy" was in fact a little girl. Her guardian had the sense to try to protect the child by dressing her as a boy.

The Story of Sau Chun

In 1899 Margarita inspected a brothel in Spofford Alley. The madam tried to keep her out, but Margarita was within her legal rights and she made her way in. None of the prostitutes requested a rescue but before Margarita left she spotted a tiny 4-year-old girl in a back curtained room. She would have taken the child with her then and there but the brothel owner, whose name was Kim Yook, claimed to be Chun's mother.

Margarita did not believe Yook for a second. The children in brothels were nearly always the children of dead prostitutes. Brothel owners raised these babies until they were old enough to be sold to local families as servants. But she could not prove that Yook was not the little girl's mother. She had to leave the child there, but she could not forget Chun's pale little face.

Margarita asked her Salvation Army friends to look after Chun for her and make sure the child was not mistreated or sold. She never stopped praying for Chun.

For a year the Salvation Army visitors reported that Chun was as well as a child could be in that squalid environment. But then came the bad news: little Chun was very sick. The brothel owner Kim Yook still insisted she was the mother but the police made her give over the girl to the Salvation Army for nursing. The Salvation Army promised the woman that Chun would not be taken far.

Margarita was in touch with the Salvation Army nurse. As soon as Chun recovered, Kim Yook went to the little house, grabbed Chun and took her back to the darkness of the brothel. Margarita had had enough. She investigated the whole sorry affair and found proof that this woman had bought Chun for $100 when the girl was just two years old. Five-year old Sau Chun was a debt slave and would be put to work as a servant and later as a brothel girl until she died. Armed with this proof Margarita decided to rescue the child.

But she could not do it alone. The Methodist and Presbyterian rescuers often engaged the police to help them on raids, but since Chun's legal status was uncertain the police declined to help. Making matters worse, the brothel owner expected a rescue attempt and had put in extra guards. Margarita began looking for men who would help her with the rescue. She was given the name of a Mr. Francis J. Kane. He had been deputized by the San Francisco police department as a "Special" and had helped rescue girls for Donaldina Cameron and the Presbyterian mission. This would be his first rescue attempt for the Methodist Mission.

In the late morning of December 11, 1900, Frank Kane entered the home, flashed his Special badge and took little Chun from Kim Yook. He brought the child to Margarita at the Methodist Home. The rescue went so well that Kane accompanied them again on another child rescue just a few weeks later. Margarita expected a lawsuit from the determined Kim Yook. But the attack came from a completely unexpected quarter: Kane himself.

The problem began when Kane was arrested after a rescue for another group. Being arrested for rescue work was not unusual. But this time Kane and his crew cursed at the police, punched them and threw furniture.

The Methodist women were shocked to discover that not only was Kane arrested for assaulting police officers, he had also been relieved of his deputy status some months before for violent behavior. He had also been charged for kidnapping and contempt of court in several other supposed "rescue" cases. They turned out to be "child stealing" cases where Kane took a child from her parent or guardian and sold her to his employer. Kane was not convicted of these crimes, but the damage was done, and the Methodists and Presbyterians dropped him from their rescue helper rolls.

Margarita hoped that this was the end of the sordid story. But it was just the beginning, for Kane had every intention of profiting from his rescue of little Sau Chun. Kane demanded that he take custody of Sau Chun from the Methodist Mission because he had visited the Superior Court and had himself declared the legal guardian of the little girl.

He claimed that he had done it because the Methodist Home housed women of ill repute and sold them to Chinese men. In a court document Kane wrote that the Home was impacting Sau Chun whose "mind and morals [were] in danger of corruption in the Home…. The Home is a bargain counter for Chinese females rescued from brothels at the request of Chinamen who wished them taken to the Home so that ultimately they would fall into their hands."

Margarita knew that the Home was very careful about placing their rescued girls in Christian families or with respectable husbands. Given Kane's history, she suspected that Kane was being paid for his efforts to get Sau Chun back. She just did not know who was paying him. Yet.

A little over a month after Kane claimed Chun's guardianship, the Mission staff was summoned to court. The brothel owner Kim Yook was suing both the Home and Kane for guardianship, claiming that Chun was her child. The judge denied her claim and directed that the child stay at the Methodist Home, although Kane retained his legal guardianship.

This happened in January 1901. They heard nothing more from Kane for the next six months but during this time an odd thing happened. A man named Chan Wing wrote to Margarita. He claimed to be a respectable Chinese merchant who had read Chun's sad story in the newspapers and wanted to adopt her. He would give them a good sum of money for the child. He called it a "donation" and she called it "buying a child," so they refused him. But the matter was far from over.

The MEC had raised enough money to build a new Methodist Home with expanded quarters for the Orphanage. On its grand opening day in July 1901 many people were in attendance for the speeches and celebration.

Kane came too. He broke through the crowd, climbed the steps, interrupted the speaker and proclaimed to the gathered crowd and reporters that he intended to take Chun from them that very day. He served Margarita with court papers right then and there. The men in the crowd hustled Kane off the steps and the speeches resumed while Margarita hurried off to a quiet room to read the letter.

The letter stated that Kane was still Chun's guardian and that he meant to place her with the very same Chinese merchant they had refused. The only way that Kane could have known about the merchant's letter was if he was involved. Margarita was certain that the merchant had offered to pay Kane at least as much money as he had offered them for Chun.

Back to court they went on August 2. Chun was terrified, and she never let go of Margarita's hand. Once again, the court denied Kane the right to take Chun and remanded the child back to the Methodist Home's custody.

But the fight was far from over. Just a few months later Kane acted again. Large posters mysteriously appeared in Chinatown that accused the Methodist Home of selling the children they rescued. The Methodist Home was certain that Kane was behind it and put up their own posters saying "Neglect your children, allow them to enter dens of vice and iniquity and you will have us as well as the Law arrayed against you. Be kind to your children, keep them pure and clean and the Law will befriend you and you will have our aid and support."

Margarita was not alone in waging counter attacks against

Kane. Mrs. L. P. Williams, secretary of the WHMS Oriental Bureau, waded into the fray. She claimed to have proof that the merchant with whom Kane wished to place Sau Chun was in fact a "saloon keeper, and the consort of the woman from whom the child had been taken." Furthermore, Kane was representing the Chinese who claimed ownership of the child. She added that Kane was "irascible and quick-tempered and unfit as guardian."

Then they received a second court summons. Kane was bringing them back to Superior Court for a second try at giving little Chun to the merchant, Kim Yook's lover.

Margaret attended court in January 20013 accompanied by many of the Home's supporters and the little girl, who held tightly to her hand. In court Kane's attorney argued that Chun's mind and morals were in danger of corruption in their Methodist Home. But Mr. Monroe, the Methodist Home attorney, hammered away at Kane's shady reputation. The man had been involved in other cases where he sold his guardianship for sums of money, and Moore accused him of trying to do the same with Sau Chun.

Moore offered the proof that Mrs. Williams had dug up; that the Chinese merchant who wanted to adopt the child was no respectable merchant at all. He was a saloon keeper -- and his mistress was Chun's previous owner, the brothel madam Kim Yook. Moore accused Kane of taking their money and selling her the child.

The newspapers reported that there was a sensation among the court spectators and Kane's face turned very dark. But

Judge Coffey only looked thoughtfully at little Chun. Margaret must have gripped the child's hand even more tightly, for she knew that with the widespread hatred of the Chinese there was no certainty of winning in court -- even with the damning information they had unearthed.

Kane's lawyer quickly changed tactics and reminded the court that Kane was in fact the child's legal guardian, and that he would be willing to take her home himself to have her live with his family.

Then Judge Coffey did something that no one expected.

He stopped the debate and said, "Let's hear what the little girl says." He looked at Sau Chun and gently said, "Come here little one." Chun was so frightened she could hardly walk, so Margarita brought her to the Judge by the hand. Margarita stayed there while the Judge reached out his big hand and took the little girl's trembling hand in his own. "Do you want to go home with Mr. Kane, my child?" he said.

"No," Chun wailed.

"He has a nice home in San Rafael, and he has some nice little boys and girls of his own. Wouldn't you like to play with them?"

Then Chun ducked her little head under his arm and put her head on his lap. Another white man might have thrown her off, but this Judge did not move. The child's eyes filled with tears as she begged the Judge not to send her with Kane.

"Do you want to stay with me?" asked His Honor kindly.

"Oh, I want to go home," cried the little girl. "I want to go home." Judge Coffey looked up at Margaret. "And so you shall," he said. He immediately rescinded Kane's guardianship and granted it to the Mission Home instead, and bade them go home and raise the child well. They did.

The Devil Came Down to Chinatown

Part 3: Nothing Will Ever be the Same

The Devil Came Down to Chinatown

The City Falls

Not in history has a modern imperial city been so completely destroyed. San Francisco is gone. Nothing remains of it but memories and a fringe of dwelling-houses on its outskirts. Its industrial section is wiped out. Its business section is wiped out. Its social and residential section is wiped out. The factories and warehouses, the great stores and newspaper buildings, the hotels and the palaces of the nabobs, are all gone. Remains only the fringe of dwelling houses on the outskirts of what was once San Francisco. (Author Jack London)

Chinatown sounded very exotic to American ears. It had shops, stores full of Chinese goods, restaurants, drug stores, gambling dens, opium cellars, brothels, pagan temples, and more than 15,000 Chinese.

And on a Wednesday morning of April 18, 1906, Chinatown ceased to exist.

A devastating earthquake and subsequent firestorm destroyed Chinatown. With it went 80% of the city of San Francisco. The earthquake of 1906 remains one of the top three worst natural disasters in the U.S. along with the horrific Galveston hurricane of 1900 and 2005's Hurricane Katrina. The earthquake holds top billing as the deadliest natural disaster in California.

Modern seismologists estimate that the earthquake

measured 7.8 on the Richter scale. The storied San Andreas fault ruptured along 267 miles if its length. The powerful earthquake contorted the earth: visible ruptures opened in a nearly 300-mile path, and the Salinas River shifted its mouth by a full 6 miles south of its original position.

The precursor was a strong foreshock that struck San Francisco and surrounding regions about 10 minutes after 5:00 am on a Wednesday morning. It shook people out of their beds but was not strong enough to do major damage. People must have breathed a sigh of relief when the shock was over; some pulled the covers back up and others got up to start their day.

Twenty-five seconds after the foreshock the real earthquake struck. The violent shaking began at 5:12 a.m. and lasted 42 seconds. The devastating quake -- followed by an even more disastrous fire -- killed 3000 people and destroyed 80% of the once-flourishing city. Initial reports put the number of fatalities at 374 white people; deaths in Chinatown and other immigrant neighborhoods were not recorded. Modern estimates put the total death toll from the quake and fires at 3000. This is a conservative number.

The great novelist Jack London was in San Francisco during the earthquake. He reported, "The streets were humped into ridges and depressions, and piled with the debris of fallen walls. The steel rails were twisted into perpendicular and horizontal angles. The telephone and telegraph systems were disrupted. And the great water mains had burst. All the shrewd contrivances and safeguards of man had been thrown out of gear by thirty seconds' twitching of the earth-crust."

Over half of San Francisco's residents were left homeless. San Francisco had a population of 410,000, and as many as 300,000 people were forced to leave their crumbling and burned-out homes. Hundreds of thousands of refugees fled the fires, overloading the ferries that crossed the Bay to Berkeley and Oakland. Some of them had friends and relatives in houses that were still standing. Many more threw up tents on beaches, Golden Gate Park and the Presidio. Eleven tent cities quickly rose.

The Army command at the nearby Presidio responded immediately, and a detachment of sailors from Chicago who were in port also reported for duty. So did the San Francisco National Guard. Immediately after the earthquake ended, National Guardsmen of the local 1st Infantry Regiment and one battalion of Coast Artillery reported to their armories. By 8:00 that morning four hundred officers and enlisted men of the San Francisco National Guard command were in place. By the end of the first day, the entire Guard was mobilized, and more than a thousand Guardsmen were on hand to help the fire department, the Army and the fleeing civilians. About 4,000 Army troops were also on duty in the city from the day of the quake to July 1, 1906, when civilians resumed control. In April 27, 1906 the *San Francisco Call* praised the Guard in an editorial.

"In the emergency that fell upon San Francisco the National Guard was immediately indispensable. It was a situation quite beyond the police. The Regulars within instant reach were few. The warships were at a distance.... But Governor Pardee at once threw the National Guard into the streets of the city, and there, facing all the risk of a battle, and more, doing all duty and more, for they manned engines and fought fire, the National Guard preserved order, restrained the prowling and dishonest, succored and protected the fire refugees and held the situation in hand until the augmentation of the regular forces."

San Francisco's Grand Opera House attracted top performers from around the country. Tenor Enrico Caruso and members of New York City's Metropolitan Opera Company came to San Francisco to perform. The night before the earthquake, Caruso performed *Carmen*. Afterwards he slept in his suite in the Palace Hotel. On Wednesday morning he was awakened by the violent shaking of the great earthquake. He grabbed up his most precious possession -- an autographed picture of President Theodore Roosevelt -- and fled the doomed city. The Met members all made it out, but their traveling costumes and props did not. Caruso never returned to San Francisco.

Mrs. Emma Burke later wrote about her and her husband's immediate experience with the quake.

"It was 5:13 a.m., and my husband had arisen and lit the gas stove, and put on the water to heat. He had closed our bedroom door that I might enjoy one more nap... The shock came, and hurled my bed against an opposite wall. I sprang up, and, holding firmly to the foot-board managed to keep on my feet to the door. The shock was constantly growing heavier; rumbles, crackling noises, and falling objects already commenced the din."

She tried to get out of the bedroom but the door was jammed shut, wedged deep into the door frame by the force of the quake. Her husband was trying to get it open from the other side, but it stood fast until an aftershock rolled through and the building twisted in the opposite direction.

> "It grew constantly worse, the noise deafening; the crash of dishes, falling pictures, the rattle of the flat tin roof, bookcases being overturned, the piano hurled across the parlor, the groaning and straining of the building itself, broken glass and falling plaster, made such a roar that no one noise could be distinguished."

The couple and their son clung to their bedroom doorways as the chimney came crashing through the floor and a heavy picture weighing over one hundred pounds crashed down from the wall less than 8' away from them. The floor moved like water: short, choppy waves like a trembling ocean. "I never expected to come out alive," Emma wrote. "I looked across the reception-room at the white face of our son, and thought to see the floors give way with him momentarily. How a building could stand such motion and keep its frame intact is still a mystery to me."

The shaking lasted 48 seconds.

The Fires

In the quiet of the city after the shaking stopped, an even

more destructive force was brewing. Much of the water supply came to the city in rigid iron pipes and about 30,000 pipes ruptured with the intense shaking. The fires began immediately, starting in the working-class neighborhoods and factories from lanterns, forges, candles and stoves. It was fed by broken gas mains and large Pacific Gas & Electric storage tanks that twisted and broke in the quake. PG &E

By Wednesday afternoon winds came howling into the city from all four directions. Witnesses reported that just outside the city the wind was dead calm. Inside the city, heated air rising from the fires sucked in the wind as if it were a giant taking an unending breath.

Fire Chief Dennis Sullivan was an expert on the use of dynamite to set back fires and destroy structures to act as fire breaks. But Sullivan was killed in the initial quake. His assistant chiefs called for help to the army at the Presidio who agreed that they must set off explosions to destroy threatened buildings to create fire breaks. The fire department and army primarily used dynamite.

Captain Le Vert Coleman of the Presidio Artillery Corps later reported on the dangerous work. "The charges often had to be laid in buildings already on fire; the dynamite had to be carried by hand through showers of sparks; the wires constantly shortened by repeated explosions, could be replaced only by climbing poles in the burning district and cutting down street wires."

The plan was a high-risk move as the dynamite multiplied the fires and burned more and more neighborhoods. Near the end of the four-day burning spree, their efforts may finally have created fire breaks. But between the burning gas mains, the explosions, and the broken water mains, nearly 30,000 structures burned across 75% of the city.

Looting was a problem on Wednesday. In her diary, dentist Leonie von Zesch wrote that she and her mother, a German countess, walked through the city's high-end shopping district following the quake and before the fire reached the area.

> "We saw the plate glass show windows of the City of Paris slivered on the sidewalk so that beautiful handmade lingerie and the finest table linens lay within arm's reach, a half block on each street. The same at the White House. Hugenin's, a custom jewelry shop, was equally exposed. It was a paradise for shoplifters until later in the day when soldiers took severe measures to stop looting."

The severe measures were Mayor E Schmitz's "Shoot to Kill" order for looters, giving the right to use deadly force to federal troops and the police. One Captain Edward Ord wrote to his mother and bitterly accused some soldiers in his 22nd Infantry of doing the looting themselves. But he did allow that most of the soldiers served well and honorably to maintain security in the city.

Dr. von Zesch and her mother continued their tour. Leonie wrote:

> "By the time we had made our way down to the Call, Examiner and Chronicle Buildings, the exodus

from the south was in full swing because there the fire had already started. Vehicles of all descriptions carried all kinds of people and what seemed to be the most dilapidated chattels they owned. Panic-stricken humans make strange choices - parrots and canaries, dogs and cats, ducks and chickens. Tottering old men, uncombed, unwashed and ragged, led equally tottering old women. One hugged a puppy to her chest and he had a kitten hanging from a coat pocket, their belongings tied in a red handkerchief."

At 1:00 a.m. early Thursday morning Jack London walked through the deserted downtown before the fires swept through.

"Everything still stood intact," he wrote. "There was no fire. And yet there was a change. A rain of ashes was falling. The watchmen at the doors were gone. The police had been withdrawn. There were no firemen, no fire-engines, no men fighting with dynamite. The district had been absolutely abandoned. I stood at the corner of Kearney and Market, in the very innermost heart of San Francisco. Kearny Street was deserted. Half a dozen blocks away it was burning on both sides. The street was a wall of flame. And against this wall of flame, silhouetted sharply, were two United States cavalrymen sitting their horses, calming watching. That was all. Not another person was in sight. In the intact heart of the city two troopers sat their horses and watched."

Pockets of Resistance

One neighborhood was apparently saved due to the residents' large wine collections. Telegraph Hill was right in the way of the rushing fire. The Italian immigrants gathered on top of the hill with all the water they could get their hands on -- and the many barrels of wine that were aging in their basements. The liquid deluge kept the flames from climbing the hill and the neighborhood was spared.

In another story of survival, San Francisco was the home to the largest collection of plants in the Western U.S. The collection was housed at the herbarium of the California Academy of Sciences in San Francisco. The Academy withstood the earthquake, but fire threatened the building. The Curator of Botany, the heroic Alice Eastwood, saved nearly 1,500 specimens of plant life including exceptionally rare and newly discovered species. She and her assistants toted the precious collection out of the city with the fire licking at their heels.

But most of the city and its possessions were doomed. Reverend Ng Poon Chew was the founder and editor of Chinatown's *Chung Sai Yat Po* and an ordained minister in the Chinese Presbyterian Church. "The gases, the smoke, the cinders, the copper sun, the haze, made it a hideous dream," he later recalled.

Through the Burning Streets

The fire made no distinction between Chinese and white, rich and poor. Thursday morning at 5:15 a.m., Jack London found himself briefly resting on the top of the steps of a home in Nob Hill, the exclusive neighborhood of San Francisco's millionaires. With him sat Japanese, Italians, Chinese, and blacks. The gathering was strangely peaceful but short-lived. To the east and south two walls of flame were inexorably advancing toward the enclave.

A famous family name -- Stanford, Huntington, Colton -- was no ward against the fires, and the mansions burned as surely as the wooden structures of Chinatown. Witnesses from around the city watched the burning on the third day. First the roofs began to smoke, and then pillars of fire shot into the roiling smoke clouds above.

Finally, all that the people could see were the flames. The fires eventually destroyed 490 city blocks, 2,830 acres, 30 schools, 80 churches, and a total of 28,000 properties. Among the destroyed churches was the First Chinese Baptist Church. (Today's building was built on the ruins of the first church in 1908. The builders deliberately used some of the bricks from the original building in the new one.)

The residents of Chinatown received word that fire was headed straight for their quarter. The dead were left behind, and 15,000 Chinese made the trek on foot towards safety.

The Reverend Nam-Art Soo Hoo and his family were among them. He was the Presbyterian Church's first ordained Chinese pastor in Chinatown. After the quake and with the fires quickly approaching, he knew that he and his family had to make for the Bay ferries bound for Oakland.

He quickly organized his wife, children and immediate

neighbors into five groups. Knowing that each group would have to deal with local authorities he made sure that each one had at least one member who spoke English. His own group consisted of his three children, his wife, and a neighboring mother with her two little children. The neighbor's feet were bound, and she could only move slowly.

The pastor told his oldest child, a 14-year-old daughter, that she must at all costs watch out for her younger brother and sister. The small groups started off. But in the crush and confusion, the pastor's three children were separated from their parents.

In later years his youngest daughter remembered, "We saw many people crushed and mangled, and tried to extricate them. There were many houses with one or two sides gone--but the furniture inside still there, before being consumed by the fire, like open doll-houses -- but there was the feeling of being lost and forgotten, for it was three days before we were able to get on a ferry boat to cross the Bay."

The children prayed constantly for help, and God answered. The 14-year-old brought her little brother and sister safely to Oakland. The children finally reunited with their frantic parents at the Chinese refugee camp.

Jack London wrote about the mass evacuation of Wednesday night.

"Before the flames, throughout the night, fled tens of thousands of homeless ones. Some were wrapped in blankets. Others carried bundles of bedding and dear household treasures. Sometimes a whole family was harnessed to a carriage or delivery wagon that was weighted down with their possessions. Baby buggies, toy wagons, and go-carts were used as trucks, while every other person was dragging a trunk. Yet everybody was gracious. The most perfect courtesy obtained. Never in all San Francisco's history, were her people so kind and courteous as on this night of terror."

A resident whose home survived remembered that first day.

"Many burned-out people passed our house with bundles and ropes around their necks, dragging heavy trunks. From the moment they heard that fatal, heart-rending sound of the trumpet announcing their house would be burned or dynamited, they had to move on or be shot. As the sun set, the black cloud we watched all day became glaringly red, and indeed it was not the reflection of our far-famed Golden Gate sunset."

San Francisco resident Mrs. Burke summed up the devastation she saw on the fourth day.

"Yesterday we rode in an old vegetable wagon, down through the devastated city, to the Ferry Building. Familiar places could be located only by the few towering steel structures, rising gaunt and bare over heaps of brick and stone, tangled wires, warped metal girders, and remnants of tottering walls. Verily the abomination of desolation, and four square miles of it -- the great, pulsing commercial heart of the town in ashes."

The Methodist Mission's Fate

"Then, turning back to snatch a baby from her crib, I heard another child screaming, who had been left alone in the room, and snatched her up; and got down the stairs I shall never know how!" (Carrie G. Davis)

By 1903, the new immigration station at Angel Island had slowed the flow of illegal Chinese immigration. However, well-placed bribes still brought in 30-40 Chinese women on each freighter. Carrie G. Davis had become the new Supervisor of the Methodist Mission. She enthusiastically embarked on a program of educating her young charges and of stopping slave smuggling right at San Francisco's docks.

The Pacific Mail shipping company ran most American freighters between the West Coast and Asia. They were also the ships who took steerage passengers on from China; many of them kidnapped or defrauded young women bound for the slave trade in San Francisco.

Once the exhausted girls arrived they found that there were no husbands waiting for them and no good jobs. Instead there were white men who met them and told them they were here to help them find their husbands. These men rounded up the women and escorted them firmly off the dock to a lonely patch of land between empty warehouses. Then Chinese men came, and money passed between the men to the tune of $900 per girl

-- a lot of money in those days. Most of those girls vanished into the darkness of the brothel alleyways forever.

Carrie Davis kept the shipping schedule of every Pacific Mail freighter going between San Francisco and points east. When a ship arrived, she was already waiting on the dock, and as the young Chinese women began filing down the gangplank she loudly informed them in rough Cantonese that evil men would make slaves of them and that she was here to take them to safety. Some of the girls were too cowed to resist or too certain that husbands were waiting for them, but some girls chose to come with Carrie back to the Methodist Home.

Early on the morning of the earthquake, Superintendent Carrie Davis slept the sleep of the just. All was well at the Methodist Home. Then, at 5:00 in the morning, the first shaking began. Carrie awakened from a sound sleep and lay in bed clutching the covers as she waited for it to stop. It did after half a minute. She got up to make sure the children were all right when the real earthquake began. Carrie later wrote:

> "Owing to the violent pitching of the house, I was thrown back into bed twice on attempting to get out. I finally succeeded in reaching the outside door of my room, and in the midst of crashing glass, falling chimneys and plaster, and cracking of the walls, I called loudly for the women and children to get downstairs and out on the street. Then, turning back to snatch a baby from her crib, I heard another child screaming, who had been left alone in the room, and snatched her up; and got down the stairs I shall never know how!"

Carrie and the older girls and women grabbed up toddlers and babies and made it safely out of the rocking house. Carrie counted heads: 48 women and children plus several women on the staff. Everyone had made it safely to the street. After a little while Carrie ventured back into the house. She took a few staff members with her and told them to wait in the entry hall while she hurried upstairs. She grabbed up handfuls of clothing and shoes from the dorms. Standing on the second story landing, she threw them downstairs into the hallway below. The staff hurled them outside and the waiting girls quickly pulled their dresses on over their nightclothes.

Carrie made one more dash into her office to take the Home's most important records and the cash, for she had no idea when they would return. She then ran back into the street with the heavily damaged Methodist Home collapsing right behind her. The girls stood together in the street holding hands and praying. Carrie quoted from the 91st psalm: "He shall cover thee with his feathers; and under his wings shalt thou take refuge."

The old wooden chapel was still standing next door. It creaked alarmingly in the aftershocks and Carrie did not take shelter there, but she led in a small group of the older girls to gather a few more belongings. Several of the girls snatched up their Bibles.

They were not alone on the Chinatown street. Most of the apartment buildings had emptied out as walls and roofs shook down around people's ears. There was little panic at this point, but people excitedly exchanged news.

Carrie was not certain where to take the girls, so she stayed put along with most of the Chinese milling about in the street. But a few hours later the word came that fires had struck the city and were burning out of control. Carrie wrote, "But we thought nothing of it, as it was in another part of the city, and we had no idea that it would reach us, and even when it crossed the city, and burned but six blocks below us, I did not feel that it could possibly take our Mission."

But during the afternoon one of the Mission supporters made his way to the front of the Mission. Mr. Bovard and his wife had tried to reach the Mission that morning. They took the ferry across the Bay but when they landed the streets leading into the city were all on fire. Mr. Bovard sent his wife back to safety and then walked a wide berth around the burning city for 9 miles before finding his way to the Mission. The entire time he feared what he would find.

The Long, Hot Journey

Bovard was overjoyed to find the Mission staff and residents safe. He told Carrie that the fire was burning within two blocks of the Mission and that they had to go. He had not come through the streets and did not know a safe path to follow, but she could hire a team of rescuers for fifty dollars to take their group beyond the fire limits. Carrie stiffened with surprise and then broke into laughter. Fifty dollars was the exact amount she had snatched from her office before she abandoned the crumbling Methodist Home. She thanked God again and prayed over her charges. With Bovard's help they quickly arranged an escort and prepared to leave.

The older children and women carried small bundles in their hands and several of them held the babies and toddlers. At Carrie's direction the rescue team led them through rubble-strewn streets to a Methodist Mission supporter's home. Mrs. Williams welcomed all of them into her small house. Brovard returned to his own home to care for his family and to share the news that the Mission residents were safe for now. All Wednesday night, while the women and girls slept crowded together on the floor, a local Chinese pastor sat in a chair by the door. His club was at hand ready to defend the house against looters.

On Thursday morning friends and neighbors arrived at the little house with terrible news. During the night the whole of Chinatown had burned to the ground. The Home and Mission buildings burned along with it, and the fires were heading this way. The only safe place left in San Francisco was on the opposite side of the Bay.

Carrie and her charges had to reach the ferry port, but it was several miles away through crumbling streets and burning buildings. The rescue teams of yesterday had fled the city. The entire household got down on their knees to pray. There was little food in the house split among 50 people. The women and children had a few crackers and oranges slices and a few drinks of water. At 7:00 they started their long journey through the smoldering city.

In a few hours they reached the Black Point area where they found many other refugees from Chinatown. Most of them had nothing but the clothes on their backs, but one Chinese man distributed a box of crackers and drinks of water among the children. Carrie blessed him for his kindness and later wrote more about her experience.

"We soon set off again. The remainder of our journey now lay under a broiling sun and the terrible heat of the burning city. A braver band of children could not be found than they were that day as they marched through the baking city. Not a child cried nor fretted, or complained. There were little four-year olds who walked all these weary miles, and the perspiration ran down their little red faces, burned with the excessive heat. Yet these little ones never once cried or fretted, not even the babies, though doing without their bottles of milk. It brought tears to my eyes to see their fortitude."

They reached the ferry port at 4 p.m.

"Thanks be to God, we reached the ferry and it was with thankful hearts we sank on a seat on the boat. From our position of safety we watched the fire devouring block after remaining block of that once-proud city. I remembered the great verse 'The angel of the lord encampeth round about them that fear him,' and I felt he was surely with us that day. All of this made us thank God and take courage to go forward."

The Presbyterian Mission Falls

"I quickly dressed and ran into the street, the building across from our place collapsed. The streets were buckling and people were running around shouting 'aih yah, dai loong jen, aih yah dai loong jen' (the earth dragon is wriggling). Later the fire came, people watched in horror as it came closer to Chinatown." (15-year-old Hugh Liang)

At the Presbyterian Home on the night before the earthquake, Donaldina and the girls were busy preparing for the Mission's annual meeting on Wednesday. Several prominent Board members were already there to spend the night including the Occidental Board Director Mrs. Browne and Board members Mrs. Wright and Mrs. Robbins.

The girls helped the staff to clean and decorate, and rehearsed the hymns they planned to sing for the meeting's attendees. Although no one knew it that night, the rehearsal would be the Home's requiem. Donaldina later wrote:

"So much has been written and said about the events that took place on that memorable eighteenth of April and the days following that it seems unnecessary to repeat an account of those occurrences. We only aim to leave a few words of testimony to bear witness in coming years to the kind care of a loving heavenly Father, and also to the unselfish courage displayed by our Chinese girls throughout the terrifying and distressing experiences of the days in which our city and the Home we loved were wiped out of existence."

When the earthquake struck in the early morning of April 18, 1906 the Mission Home rolled like ocean waves. Chimneys crashed down on the roof and through the floors, and the plaster walls crumbled and slid. Women and children screamed as they clung for dear life to whatever safety they could find. As soon as the adults and older girls could get to their feet they flew to the toddlers and babies to shield them from the falling shards of roof and wall.

Miraculously the building did not collapse even though its chimneys had crashed down to the ground. It was a 5-story building made of bricks and stood on the slope of a steep sand hill. By all rights it should have fallen like the neighboring buildings did. But the main sections of walls and roof stood fast. Once the first great shock had passed, the Mission residents thanked God for sparing their lives. They looked out the broken windows to their neighbors. The quake had reduced buildings to rubble and columns of smoke were rising through the air.

The first order of business was to get the girls dressed and fed in case they had to leave quickly. Donaldina, her staff and the Board members quickly fetched clothes and shoes and the entire group got dressed together on the first floor. Breakfast was harder since every chimney had crashed down, taking the cooking hearths and ovens with them. This problem was solved by a mission matron named Miss Ferree. As soon as she could stand after the earthquake struck, she ran to a nearby bakery that still stood and told the frightened baker to fill a big basket with as much bread as it could hold. A Chinese neighbor, Mrs. Ng Poon Chew, had the kindness to send over some apples and a kettle of tea. This was to be the last meal in the Mission's dining-room. Donaldina wrote, "Our girls gathered round the little white tables, sang as usual the morning hymn, then repeated the Twenty-third Psalm with more feeling and a deeper realization of its unfailing promises than ever before."

They had not finished eating when a severe aftershock struck the building. Most of them ran back upstairs to the upper floor and opened an eastern window that looked out over the crippled city.

"The small wreaths of smoke had rapidly changed into dark ominous clouds, hiding in places the bright waters of the bay. As we gazed with feelings of indefinable dread over the blocks below, there passed at full gallop a company of United States Cavalry. The city was under martial law. Turning from our post of outlook to the group of anxious questioning faces near us, we realized that the problems of the day were hourly growing more serious."

They heard a commotion from the entry hall. Donaldina flew down the stairs to meet another Board member, Mrs. Kelley, who had spent last night at her own home six miles from the Mission. After the earthquake Mrs. Kelley walked those miles through devastated streets to reach the Mission. Mrs. Kelley breathlessly reported on the ruined neighborhoods and the approaching fires. It was clear to everyone that the fires were coming too close for them to stay. The adults decided to take shelter at the First Presbyterian Church at the corner of Van Ness Avenue and Sacramento Street, which Mrs. Kelley had passed on the way to the Home. Built in 1849, the sturdy building had survived the earthquake and the fires were burning away from it. Donaldina remembered:

> "The streets in the neighborhood of the Home were fast filling with refugees from the lower parts of town who sought safety or a better view of the fires from our high hillsides. Chinatown also had begun pouring forth its hordes and even in the midst of the general calamity the ever vigilant highbinder was on the watch for his prey. To have our Chinese girls on the streets among these crowds after nightfall was a danger too great to risk. As hastily, therefore, as we could work amidst the confusion and excitement, we gathered some bedding, a little food, and a few garments together and the last of the girls left the Mission Home."

They walked several miles to the Presbyterian Church, making their slow way through the great crowd of refugees. They reached the safety of the church just before nightfall. The women were worried about the three babies under their care. Newborn Ah Ping was less than a month old. Her mother was a rescued prostitute whose health had suffered badly in her captivity, so she could not help much with the child. Another mother was in decent health but her little one was only three months old. The third was orphaned toddler Ah Chung, only eighteen months old.

The women and older girls took turns caring for the three little ones and the younger school-age children. Night had fallen when Donaldina and the Board members decided to trudge back to the Mission to say a final goodbye. But on their way, they encountered a military roadblock. The soldiers told them that they could not pass because the neighborhood would shortly be engulfed by fire. The streets all around had been evacuated and the solders themselves would soon fall back.

The women begged to be allowed to enter and promised that they would hurry. One young soldier let them pass on the strength of their promise. They hurried to the still-standing Mission and told the guard stationed there that they would only be a moment. He told them a moment was all they had. Donaldina reported, "The red glare from without lit up each familiar object in every room. The awful events occurring without were almost forgotten for the moment, while we stood in the room that used to be dear Miss Culbertson's and recalled the happy hours spent there with her, and the Chinese children whom she so loved."

Within a few minutes they ran out of time. In the next block the soldiers were setting off dynamite to stymie the advancing fire. The soldier in the street shouted at them to go. Donaldina quickly grabbed a few more papers and valuables from her desk. Then she and the other women "hurried through the hall strewn with many of our personal belongings, treasures which the Chinese girls had tried to save, but at the last had to abandon. We took a final look through the shadows of the large chapel room into the executive meeting rooms, sacred to memories of many an earnest and inspiring meeting."

The women returned to the First Presbyterian Church where their charges anxiously awaited. Just two hours later, as a dark sun rose over the burning city, the Mission fell to the flames. Yet they were still not safe from the fire, which was approaching the church from three directions. The church that had survived the quake would shortly be blown up as a firebreak.

It was past time to go. The only safe destination was the ferry port and escape over the Bay. But like Carrie Davis and the Methodist Home residents, the way led through a shattered and burning city. They had not brought much from the Mission, but many things they had brought had to be left behind. They decided to carry bedding, whatever food and water they had, Bibles, spare clothes, and valuable papers. But how would they carry the bundles when the babies had to be carried too?

The girls reminded Donaldina of the way the Chinese vegetable peddlers carried their goods: in two bundles hung from both ends of a pole. They tore up sheets for ropes and found broom handles that would serve for the poles. One person could carry two bundles this way. The girls laughed for the first time in many hours as they all learned to balance their bundles.

Everyone who could walk carried a load, even little five-year-old Hung Mooie. The little girl burst into tears at having to take the pole on her neck, but the women assured her that she was carrying two dozen eggs and that she would be able to have some when they stopped to cook. She tearfully consented to carry them.

An older girl had carefully rescued her treasure before they left the Mission: a heavy box carrying her fiancé's love letters. Donaldina urged her to leave it behind so he she could carry food or bedding in her bundle. But the girl was devastated and Donaldina relented. She later wrote:

> "Poor old Sing Ho just out of the City and County Hospital, who had recently lost the sight of one eye, staggered bravely along under a huge bundle of bedding and all her earthly possessions, which she cheerfully rolled down steep hills, and dragged up others. Two young mothers tied their tiny babies on their backs while others helped carry their bedding."

The small group of children and women, both white and Chinese left the sanctuary of the Presbyterian Church and trudged through streets crowded with new refugees fleeing the approaching fires. The streets leading to the Bay had been burned over the night before. The heat was intense, and the fires still smoldered in the charred ruins that lined their path. Thanks be to God they arrived safely at the foot of Market Street and the ferry dock. Ferries had been running night and day shepherding refugees to safely. One of the boats was about to cross the Bay to Sausalito, which was not far from the Presbyterian Seminary at San Anselmo. The women and girls could take sanctuary there.

> "We lost no time going on board. It was a

thankful though a completely exhausted company that sank down. We sat with our bundles and babies on the lower deck of the steamer, too weary to walk to the salon. But tired and homeless, knowing not where that night we were to lay our heads, our only feeling was one of gratitude for deliverance as we looked over the group of more than sixty young faces and realized how God had cared for His children."

They arrived safely at San Anselmo Seminary that night. Not a single woman or child had been lost.

Aftermath

The bedraggled group arrived exhausted but grateful to God and the welcoming men and women at the Seminary. Professors, students, and employees quickly pressed a seminary hall into service and layered bedding on the floor while cooks grabbed up as much bread and fruit as they could carry.

The children were asleep on their feet. The adults woke them enough to take a little bread and water, and sent them to sleep on the makeshift beds. The Board and staff swiftly fell asleep as well. Only Donaldina stayed up with the school professors and administrators, telling them the story of the exodus and everything she knew about the earthquake and fires.

Finally, the men insisted that she sleep, assuring her that tomorrow was enough time to decide together how to feed and house the girls, and how to reach the members of the Board who had not been with them that early Wednesday morning.

Donaldina thanked them again, prayed with them, and walked into the temporary dormitory to sleep. Then she heard crying.

She found teenaged Yuen Kim sobbing on her crumpled sheets. Donaldina thought she knew why. She sank down on the pile of bedding where the sobbing girl curled up and took her into her arms. Yuen Kim was slight and weighed little more than a child herself. She had been rescued from a brothel and was going to be one of the happy endings of which the Mission was so glad. She had fallen in love with a Christian Chinese man who had visited San Francisco all the way from his home in Cleveland. Romance bloomed, and the young couple would have been married Wednesday – the very day of the earthquake. Yuen Kim had had not complained once during their escape. But now she sobbed out to Donaldina that she did not know where Henry Lai was. He was already in San Francisco for their wedding. Was he dead? Was he searching for her? Had he given up and returned to Cleveland by any means possible?

Donaldina could not catch every word – Kim was speaking in a rush of Cantonese and broken English – but she understood enough. "Let's pray for him," she said firmly. They prayed together, and an exhausted Kim finally went back to sleep. Donaldina determined not to give up. She prayed that they would find enough roses for the wedding.

A few days passed, busy days of caring for the little ones and making plans for the near future. Donaldina was in the dorm when a voice rang out. "Yuen Kim? Kim!" A frantic young man burst into the dormitory. Yuen Kim ran right into his arms. Henry Lai had looked for Kim for days before hearing that the Mission girls had gone to San Anselmo. He had not known if his fiancée was dead or alive.

They married on April 21 in a beautiful ivy-covered chapel on the Seminary grounds. And Donaldina had found her roses. She wrote, "Just after the wedding, Mr. and Mrs. Henry Lai started for their home in Cleveland amidst showers of California roses and the best wishes of their many friends. So romance with its magic touch helped us for a time to forget our great losses."

The Devil Came Down to Chinatown

Life in the Rubble

The strange mysterious old Chinatown of San Francisco is gone and never more will be. But amidst surrounding ruin, on one consecrated spot stands a solid brick wall, unshattered by earthquake shock and unblackened by the breath of flame. Within that wall an unmarred archway still bears in stone letters the legend "Occidental Board of Foreign Missions." (Donaldina Cameron)

Ultimately more than 20,000 Chinese fled San Francisco and neighboring cities that had been hit hard by the quake. Most Chinese refugees headed to Oakland with its small Chinese quarter. It was not possible for the area to hold the influx of refugees, so those without immediate family in the area were escorted to a Chinese refugee camp. Other Chinese and white refugees headed to Berkeley, whose relief committee had quickly established an "Oriental department." The committee prepared several buildings to handle the influx of Japanese and Chinese refugees in the small Oriental district of Dwight Way. A gambling business was quickly turned into a nursery for babies and children up to six years old.

Like San Francisco and Oakland, Berkeley constructed a tent city for the refugees arriving daily. Train, ferry and steamship operators took hundreds of thousands of refugees over the next few weeks free of charge. Southern Pacific railroad transported more than 200,000 people out of the stricken city. Those who had nowhere else to go moved to one of the eleven Army tent cities.

A few of the areas inside the city were untouched by the fire and held many refugees. For once the camps were color-blind. A white couple volunteered at one of the camps. The wife later reported:

> "The day came on dusty and hot. The wind had changed, showering us with ashes and stinging our eyes with smoke from the ever-increasing fire. The line formed for cold water. Each had his turn. A man would [cut into line and ask] for a drink for his wife, and look down the long line of Americans, Japanese, Negroes, Chinese, and all sorts and degrees of men, women, and children. 'Just one cupful. It only takes a moment, and she's almost famished.' 'Yes, but that moment belongs to someone else,' replied my husband, with that fierce look from his old military days that I knew covered the softest heart in the world. And the man went to the foot of the line, and it was just an hour and a half before he came to the faucet for his pitcherful."

The Curio Keepers

Henry Lai and Yuen Kim were not the only romance to arise out of the ashes of the great fire. Wong Sun Yue was a merchant from Chinatown and Ella May Clemens was a white missionary to the Chinese living in San Francisco. They knew one another from Ella's work in Chinatown but had never spoken. After the earthquake, they both fled their Chinatown homes to go across the Bay. There the military directed them to one of the dozens of tent cities the Army constructed for the horde of refugees from the fallen city.

A few days after the earthquake they separately volunteered to man a soup kitchen in the tent city. Wong Sun Yue was already ladling out soup when Ella walked in. They recognized each other and in their relief smiled and laughed and took each other's hands. For the next weeks and months, they frequently volunteered together. Ella's sister was well-to-do and offered Ella a place to live outside of the tent city, but she found herself curiously reluctant to leave Sun Yue.

The Chinese merchant gathered all his courage in his hands. He was prepared to leave the tent city if Ella turned him down. He asked her to marry him and to his joy and relief – and great surprise – she agreed. Ella's socially prominent sister was horrified but Ella was an adult and there was little that Mrs. Harold Gould could do. And Ella pointed out to her sister that Katherine had not exactly toed the narrow line herself -- she had been a rider for the Buffalo Bill show before marrying railroad heir Howard Gould.

Sun Yue and Ella left the state to get married and returned directly after their honeymoon. Wong Sun Yue believed that Chinatown would be rebuilt, and he wanted to be there. Ella, who had spent most of her adult life working with the Chinese, agreed. They did not wait for Chinatown to be rebuilt but constructed a refugee hut from lumber provided by the Red Cross. They built it on Grant Street – or what had been Grant Street before the destruction of Chinatown. Mr. and Mrs. Wong Sun Yue Clemens prayed and believed it would be again.

They began to collect found objects buried in the rubble, and placed them in their refugee hut and in canvas tents that they erected around them. Ella came to believe that God was speaking to them through the strange formations they found in the ashes of the fire: melted coins, bottles, teacups, and more. Ella said about it, "Our collection is all that is left to history, to tell of a new city risen from the ashes." She and Wong Sun Yue built their collection into a curio shop, which they built around the refugee hut and made the hut a center for their earthquake tours. Their motto? "Relics saved from the ruins."

Many Chinese never returned at all but settled in inland in Fresno, Stockton, Napa, Sacramento. Ng Poon Chew was the editor of San Francisco's Chinese newspaper *Chung Sai Yat Po*. Following the earthquake and fire, he and his family bought a house in a white neighborhood in Oakland. The sale originally raised high anxiety in the neighborhood, but Ng Poon Chew soon observed that the situation changed for the better: "I smoked my cigar harmoniously with the men in the block, my wife talked over the back fence with the ladies and my children played with the other children in the block, and so far as I have been able to learn no one has ever been contaminated by association with the family."

San Francisco did not stand alone. Congress immediately voted $1 million in relief supplies. Private parties, businesses, and even foreign governments sent in large contributions. Food supplies arrived quickly by railroad, many of whose owners and founders had lost their Nob Hill mansions in the disaster. Relief workers and army personnel distributed food to the tent cities and food kitchens where all refugees were served a daily meal.

Over the next few weeks the army consolidated refugee encampments to eleven tent cities. The drafty tents were replaced by compact and sturdy wooden refugee huts. The refugees could rent the huts for $2 a month until they could move to a more permanent home. By 1907 most of the camps were emptied of refugees and the last of the camps closed in 1908.

The Fight for Chinatown

"San Francisco's new Chinatown is so much more beautiful, artistic, and so much more emphatically Oriental, that the old Chinatown, the destruction of which great writers and artists have wept over for two years, is not worthy to be mentioned in the same breath." (Chinatown planner Look Tin Eli)

San Francisco's races had pulled together during the quake but prejudice against the Chinese quickly reasserted itself. After a few weeks the Army was ordered to segregate the camps. The Chinese camp was moved several times due to complaints by white neighbors, and finally ended up for the next two years at the windy edge of the Presidio.

It took a year to clear all the debris-choked streets and to repair the railways. One of the earliest tracks to be repaired ran to the Marina district. Trains carried many millions of tons of debris from the city center and surrounding neighborhoods. Workers dumped the debris into pits to create a landfill and the exclusive Marina grew on top of it over the years. (It is no accident that the Marina district was severely damaged in the Loma Prieta earthquake -- it rested on the weak foundation of the debris from the 1906 earthquake.)

Meanwhile the San Franciscan powers-that-be were determined to rebuild the city as fast as they could. The mayor quickly formed a Reconstruction Committee formed of the most prominent citizens of San Francisco.

The rebuilding effort was intense. Wealthy families rebuilt their homes quickly, alumni pitched in with fund-raising efforts for the universities and colleges, and private citizens gave generously to rebuild hospitals and museums. Investment dollars poured in to rebuild proud new hotels and company offices in the swiftly rising downtown. San Franciscans were proud of their resurrecting city and supportive of the Committee's efforts.

But one big question remained -- what to do about Chinatown?

There were tens of thousands of Chinese ready to move back home but Chinatown occupied one of the most valuable pieces of real estate in the city. The fact was not lost on the politicians and investors in San Francisco, who saw their golden opportunity. Old Chinatown had been a crazy quilt of wooden buildings, garish colors, peeling paint, and narrow streets and alleys. The tinder-dry buildings had burned to ash in the fires and the section was destroyed. Why not relocate the Chinese to a less valuable neighborhood?

Most of the white businessmen on the Reconstruction Committee looked at it that way. Chinatown's prime real estate property was right next to the sparkling new downtown and they coveted it.

Some elements of the press joined in the movement. The *Overland Monthly* wrote, "Fire has reclaimed to civilization and cleanliness the Chinese ghetto, and no Chinatown will be permitted in the borders of the city ... It appears a divine wisdom directed the range of the seismic horror and the range of the fire god. Wisely, the worst was cleared away with the best."

Despite the vicious hyperbole not everyone on the planning board was behind Chinese relocation. The Rev. Filben, who had rescued Chinese prostitutes and was a crusader for Chinese rights, chaired the Relief of Chinese committee while political boss Abe Ruef chaired the Relocation of the Chinese Committee. The two frequently butted heads. Filben knew that Ruef owned a large Chinatown brothel called the Municipal Crib, and gave Mayor Schmitz generous kickbacks for looking the other way. Schmitz fully supported the plan to move Chinatown to a decidedly poorer location. They felt that the mud flats of Hunters Point were an excellent location – no one else wanted to build there and it was far from the city's center.

The Chinese Six Companies had quietly allied with the Tongs over the relocation issue. The prominent Chinese businessmen protested to the committee that:

> "I have heard the report that the authorities intend to remove Chinatown, but I cannot believe it. America is a free country, and every man has a right to occupy land which he owns provided that he makes no nuisance. The Chinese Government owns the lot on which the Chinese Consulate of San Francisco formerly stood, and this site on Stockton street will be used again. It is the intention of our Government to build a new building on the

property, paying strict attention to the new building regulations which may be framed."

The Chinese consulate was also fighting relocation. The Consul-General was in active communication with the ruler of China, the powerful Dowager Empress Tzu-hsi. The Empress, who had effectively ruled China for 45 years, was expressly not amused.

When the local Chinese representatives and the Chinese Consul General met with the city relocation committee, their worst suspicions were confirmed. The new Chinatown location was indeed to be the mud flats to the south of the city, which today is the Hunters Ridge area.

The Chinese Consul and the Six Companies mustered their arguments, and they were good ones. Much of Chinatown, they said, was made up of businesses. Each small laundry, restaurant, curio store or gambling den may not pay a high tax, but the combined taxes of hundreds of businesses enriched city coffers. And if they could not rebuild in Chinatown then surely Portland, Seattle, or even Los Angeles would be happy to welcome them. The Chinese also pointed out that the mud flats were not a part of San Francisco. The taxes would go to the county, not the city.

Consul General Yung went a step further. He was resplendent in his traditional Chinese silken robes as he reported that he had discussed the possibility of relocating Chinatown with the Dowager Empress. He fixed each white face in the room with his gaze. "The Empress is not happy about Chinatown being relocated. We intend to rebuild the

Chinese consulate in the heart of Chinatown. Where it was."

In the wake of the loss of taxes and an international incident, San Francisco's leaders relented. Shortly thereafter Mayor Schmitz and boss Abe Ruef were arrested on corruption and conspiracy charges.

The official reconstruction of Chinatown began about a year after the disaster, but one building already stood. A Chinese merchant named Look Tin Eli did not wait for the official word but designed and rebuilt his Sing Chong Bazaar in an Americanized Chinese style to appear exotic, colorful and attractive to tourists: "an Oriental city of veritable fairy palaces." The exciting new building stood on the corner of California and Grant streets where it loomed in front of visitors.

Look Tin Eli and Lew Hing founded Canton Bank specifically to make loans for Chinatown's redevelopment, fearing that white banks would make loans at killing interest rates. More Chinese and white businessmen quickly followed Look Tin Eli's lead. New Chinatown rose from the ashes like a garish phoenix in red, gold and green colors, pagoda roofs and dragons. The flashiest stores rebuilt first closely followed by the banks and the hospital, then the Tongs' and Six Companies' headquarters buildings.

The Missions Rebuild

"We had to find a place for our young women and girls but due to the displaced population of San Francisco, there were few rentals to be had. Even then most landlords refused to rent to Chinese. Finally we found temporary quarters that we needed to rebuild the Methodist Home." (Carrie Davis)

The Presbyterians quickly rebuilt their Mission in a different location in Chinatown. Donaldina wrote, "To mention the names of all the good and generous friends who have helped by sympathy, by gifts, and with money, would require the writing of another story."

But the Methodist Mission struggled to find a new home. They found temporary quarters at 2116 Spaulding Avenue in Berkeley. The property was surrounded by several acres of vacant land that was a safety buffer against the highbinders. Carrie wrote, "Unlike the Methodist Home in San Francisco, there was no one to molest us or make us afraid, since we are far removed from any of the [highbinders]. We live a very quiet life and there is a beautiful view of the hills and the bay."

Yet despite the beautiful and safe surroundings, they could not stay for long. Donations of clothing and shoes had poured in to the Mission group but there was little else in the house. Carrie said that although she told people that the girls had beds to lie on; the beds consisted of clothing rolled up on the floor and cots for the younger or sick girls. "Pillows, sheets, pillow covers, spreads, towels, table covers, napkins, knives and forks, teaspoons, tablespoons--anything and everything needed in a home--will be received with great gratitude. We are simply in a house with nothing in it."

In a year almost nothing had changed. The girls were in the same poorly furnished house and they lived hand to mouth. Mrs. F.D. Bovard was the secretary of the Bureau for Chinese Work and was responsible for the Mission staff and girls' wellbeing. She resigned in a letter where she scolded the church for not giving to build a new Mission.

"There is no gas or electricity, and little or no prospect of getting it. The matron [Miss Lois Thorn] broke down because no one could be found to relieve her, for a vacation and rest. Since then it has been impossible to find a matron because of the cramped quarters for workers (who share the same bedroom) and the general inconvenience of the house arrangements. The superintendent is alone with the girls."

The landlord agreed to remodel Spaulding House to make it more welcoming to its occupants, but only if the Bureau for Chinese Work would sign a long-term lease. This they refused to do since the WHMS women felt strongly that the Home should return to a rebuilt Chinatown. Carrie and the girls wanted this too but there was simply no money to rebuild. Fervent prayers seemed to go unanswered. In 1907 Carrie appealed to the national WHMS. "We must have the Home rebuilt at once. . . . We pray that our friends will come to the rescue and take a part in the new Home that is to be."

The issue was not so much the amount of donations. MEC members gave generously to the WHMS and intended their donation to go to rebuilding the Home. But there was some uncertainty over who controlled the money: the MEC's Board of Home Missions and Church Extension, or the Woman's Home Missionary Society. Some funds were released, enough to build a kindergarten in new Chinatown. But the Presbyterians had already rebuilt their Mission in Chinatown and the WHMS women in San Francisco were increasingly frustrated.

Finally, financial negotiations between WHMS and the MEC Mission Board bore fruit. Mrs. Julia Piatt had replaced the exhausted Mrs. Brovard as the Bureau Secretary and announced to the WHMS national meeting that, "The matter of the property adjustment between the Board of Home Missions and Church Extension and the Woman's Home Missionary Society has finally been settled." She added that "the erection of our building will proceed at once, and the delayed and long-talked of Methodist Home will soon be a realized force for salvation expressed in brick and mortar."

But there was still not enough money to rebuild. Enough funds were released to the Home's residents to move from Spaulding House into a more suitable building on University Avenue. But Carrie and Mrs. Piatt felt that there should be more, a rebuilt Home and Mission rising from the ashes of Chinatown.

A National Tour

After intense prayer Carrie decided that the WHMS would be more inclined to give if they witnessed the rescued children for themselves. She proposed that she take some children with her for a series of concerts and talks in Philadelphia. The tour coordinated with the WHMS Board of Managers meeting and was supposed to last one month. It lasted seven.

Carrie chose seven girls and one boy who could sing in English and they set out from Berkeley for Philadelphia. The meeting in the historic city lasted for eight days, and the children sang each day as Carrie talked about the great work of God through the Home and how they needed to rebuild in Chinatown. Word about the concerts at the Church of the Covenant spread throughout the city, and then went national as newspapers picked up the uplifting story.

Invitations from churches and community groups all over the country poured in to WHMS in Philadelphia. During their month-long stay there, the little group received nearly 50 invitations and Carrie accepted nearly everyone. The WHMS in San Francisco was less than thrilled at their Mission Superintendent being gone so long, but Carrie felt strongly that God would work through her and the children to raise money for rebuilding. So, raise money she would, no matter how long they had to be away.

Several of the invitations were from Washington DC, and one of those was directly from the White House. President Theodore Roosevelt's secretary wrote that the President would be charmed to hear the children from San Francisco. The little group traveled to Washington DC. The children performed for the President on November 5, 1908. President Roosevelt was delighted with the performance and requested that they sing again in the lobby for visitors and the press.

Before they went downstairs, the one boy in the tiny choir decided to speak seriously to the President about current events. Republican William Howard Taft had defeated Democrat William Jennings Bryan in the presidential election just two days before and Roosevelt was due to step down in January. The little boy folded his arms and said, "Mr. President, when I was down in Lincoln, Nebraska I was for Bryan; but since I came up here I am for Taft -- because you are."

The President laughed and told the child, "You are a politician -- and a mighty great one already."

The small choir held several performances in Washington DC, including a visit to the Chinese embassy to sing for Wu T'ing-Fang, the Chinese foreign minister to the United States. They also met with the Secretary of Commerce and Labor, Oscar Straus, who was directly responsible for carrying out the United States Chinese immigration policy. Although Congress stubbornly held to the Exclusion Act, Secretary Strauss was a leading member of the American Jewish Committee, which worked against immigration restrictions. He also knew first-hand what it was to be discriminated against – he was the first Jewish cabinet member in the history of the United States.

From Washington DC the small group headed north, then to the Midwest and to Utah. The tour was extremely successful but with the long travel Carrie's health began to suffer, and some of the children came down with measles in Salt Lake City. They also had more invitations in the West than they could do.

By the time they returned to California, Carrie and one of the girls were briefly hospitalized.

Nevertheless, Carrie and the WHMS considered the tour to be richly blessed by God and a great success. Relieved at having the children and Superintendent back in one piece, Mrs. Piatt of the WHMS Board reported, "The visit of Miss Davis and the eight children through the East was a revelation to many of our people and did more to really interest and awaken the members of the Woman's Home Missionary Society to the merits of our work than any other method we could have employed. During the seven months of their travel they visited forty-two cities, and many thousands of people outside of our Society learned something of the work of the Woman's Home Missionary Society as it is carried on under the Bureau for Chinese Work on the Pacific Coast. Lasting friends were made for the work, and we are hoping great things from them. The results of that trip we cannot estimate, but we trust we will go on reaping benefits from it in ever-increasing volumes of sympathy and love and generous gifts."

More gifts for the rebuilding of the Home steadily streamed in. But Carrie paid for the intense seven-month trip when she had a physical and emotional breakdown shortly after her return to San Francisco. Yet despite her failing health she was glad.

"We cannot begin to tell of all the splendid achievements of this trip. . . . making known in colleges, universities, high schools, Bible Schools, kindergartens, clubs and churches of every denomination, YWCA and YMCA, and private homes -- the story of our labor of love among and for these people under the Woman's Home Missionary Society on the Pacific Coast. It was a strenuous trip, yet made plain to us that God was with us: Never a stop or hindrance or accident to ourselves or the train we were on. Never late or one of our engagements broken because of weather or sickness. Called to go places we never expected, raising thousands of dollars for our new Home and the work. Converting many to missions, putting a love for the Home work as well as the foreign work into the hearts of others. Hearing splendid men of our church say, 'Nothing you could have ever done could have made such a demonstration of missions as this has.' And hearing them say, 'If this is what the WHMS is doing, come into our churches and we will open both our pocketbooks and our hearts to you.'"

Before they could begin building they had to solve legal disputes over the site of the Mission's original Washington Street lot. They won the court case and started to rebuild on Washington Street in 1909. But the case had drained their funds and there was not enough money to complete the new Mission.

Carrie was still in poor health when she decided that God wanted her to travel back to Buffalo, New York in 1910 to meet with the WHMS Board of Managers. She pronounced the trip a success thanks to the Lord's guidance. "This trip financially was far beyond my expectations, and indeed every other way and again we could see that the Lord was leading us, and giving us success." With the new funds in place, work began again on the building and in December 1911 a lovely new Methodist Home had literally risen from the ashes at 940 Washington Street.

Carrie's health grew progressively worse due to the strain of the earthquake, travel and rebuilding. In the spring of 1913 she was visiting Spokane, Washington when she broke down again. She had to leave the Mission and the work that she loved, and lived quietly until 1925 when she died after a prolonged illness. She was sixty-eight years old, and like Margaret Culbertson before her she died a martyr to her work.

Legacy

"Because of the faithfulness and courage of the millions of women who prayed, planned, organized, marched, petitioned, labored, and supported the work of the early missionary societies, the lives of countless individuals, especially women and children, have been irrevocably changed. Women, children and youth in our generation, and the ones that will follow us, are living the legacy of the women's missionary movement of the 19th century." (The United Methodist Women 30th celebration)

The work of the Presbyterian Chinese Mission Home continued until 1939. Donaldina Cameron never forgot her mission. As a popular figure in the public eye, she could keep the rescues of Chinese slave girls front and center in the press and in the public's attention. But national officials in the Presbyterian Church were not as impressed. Pointing out that the number of Chinese prostitutes in San Francisco was steadily dwindling; they wanted her to scale down the immigrant work. Citing the board's earlier promise to help her build a rescue mission "permanently and adequately" -- the agreement's exact words -- she steadfastly refused to sell the Mission Home even while she searched for larger quarters for the rescue work.

In 1925 she raised enough money and interest to open a new house for Chinese girls in Oakland. She even made plans to build a new complex in San Mateo to serve immigrant Chinese women and children.

However, even the redoubtable Donaldina could not overcome the strong objections of the Rev. Hermann Nelson Morse. Rev. Morse was a Presbyterian pastor, sociologist and author who argued that the changing social factors in San Francisco had made the prostitute rescue program obsolete. Strict federal immigration laws had restricted immigration throughout the country, and San Francisco's official immigration checkpoint at Angel Island was particularly effective.

He also pointed out that the state of California was funding several institutions for abandoned and at-risk juveniles that had not existed in the heyday of the Presbyterian mission. Finally, the Rev. Morse pointed out the large amount of money that the Presbyterian mission organizations expended on Chinese work, not only in San Francisco but in most of the coastal states. Rev. Morse's studious evidence encouraged the mission officials to withdraw their support from Donaldina's expansion plans. They could not outright relieve Donaldina of her position as she had an extremely loyal personal following and was popular throughout the country. Instead they gave her a new position: lead Presbyterian rescue work across the United States and lobby for more restrictive laws against prostitution.

Donaldina announced that she was glad to take on the task since she was already active nationally. But she added that she could not possibly leave the Mission home until she found a suitable replacement as Superintendent – and she could not seem to find the right person.

By 1936 the Presbyterian Church sold the lovely Oakland Home to Mills College, feeling that it was too far away from

Oakland's Chinatown. Emboldened by the sale, they insisted that the central Home in San Francisco change from being a rescue home to a Chinese language school. Their thinking was that there were few prostitute rescues anymore and a language school would serve the Chinatown community better.

Donaldina insisted just as strongly that she had been promised permanent adequate funding for the Rescue Mission. The Board decided to investigate the Home to see if the great stories that had happened there were still happening. The investigators were hardly neutral on the matter. Dr. Frederick Payne headed up the investigation with the express purpose of making a case for the Board to give up the rescue work.

He was not entirely wrong. The doctor spoke with several civic organizations that had dealings with the Rescue Home. Of these organizations, only the Juvenile Court wanted to keep it open because they used it as a halfway house for delinquent Chinese girls. It was Payne's opinion that "we have just provided a soft basket where the Juvenile Court could dump its rubbish, at a minimum expense to the county."

The Board closed the Chinese Mission Home and appointed Lorna Logan to succeed Donaldina. In 1939 Miss Logan rented much smaller quarters on Wetmore Street to house the handful of women who still lived at the Home. Armed with this information, national officials moved to close the programs for Chinese women and girls at the Chinese Mission Home.

But God did not stop work at the passing of the Rescue Mission. Today the Cameron House serves San Francisco's

Chinatown as a Christian social services agency offering counseling, clinics, support groups, and food projects.

The Methodist Legacy

The MEC and WHMS never relinquished their Mission. Although the problem of Chinese prostitution in Chinatown changed over the years, the old Methodist Home became *Gum Moon*: "Escape from the Green Mansion" in Cantonese. Gum Moon is still affiliated with the United Methodist Church. Under the General Board of Global Ministries, Gum Moon shelters women and children and teaches adults the skills to live and thrive in San Francisco. The building has a polished stone at its entryway that is from the threshold of the original Mission house at 912 Washington Street. In the year 2002, the United Methodist Church celebrated UMW's 30th anniversary. UMW organizers wrote:

> "In the early years of the women's mission organizations, the focus was on sending missionaries and helping to change the lives of women and girls in foreign lands. They incorporated the values of home and family into public life as they addressed issues of poverty, child labor, immigration, migrant labor, family life, racial discrimination, full clergy rights for women, and many other social ills of the day.

> "Many problems faced by the women at the turn of the century have reemerged in our own time with a new and demanding urgency: new waves of immigration, homelessness, racial divisions, threats

to the environment, substance abuse and addiction, lack of affordable health care, concerns for the well-being of children and the elderly, public education, questions about women's roles in society, and world peace.

"Because of the faithfulness and courage of the millions of women who prayed, planned, organized, marched, petitioned, labored, and supported the work of the early missionary societies, the lives of countless individuals, especially women and children, have been irrevocably changed. Women, children and youth in our generation, and the ones that will follow us, are living the legacy of the women's missionary movement of the 19th century."

Christian men and women have worked together through the centuries to spread the kingdom of God throughout the earth. In the San Francisco of the 1800s and early 1900s, men and women preached the Good News of Jesus Christ to the slave and the alien. They are still doing so today as the Holy Spirit inspires us to serve out the Great Commission. May we never, ever forget.

"Therefore go and make disciples of all nations, baptizing them in the name of the Father and the Son and the Holy Spirit, teaching them to observe all that I commanded you; and lo, I am with you always, even to the end of the age." (Mt. 28:19-20)

The Devil Came Down to Chinatown

Bibliography

Missionary Herald, Vol. 17. Proceedings at large of the American Board of Commissioners for Foreign Missions. 1836.

Berson, Robin Kadison. *Marching to a Different Drummer: Unrecognized Heroes of American History.* Greenwood Press, Westport, CT. 1994.

Borthwick, J.D. *Three Years in California.* University of California, Berkeley. 1857.

Bowen, Robert W. Young Bowen, Brenda. *San Francisco's Chinatown.* Arcadia Publishing. 2008.

Californian Illustrated Magazine, Volume 1. Edited by Charles Frederick Holder, Edward James Livernash. Californian Publishing Company, 1892.

Chan Hon Fan, Letter to the Editor. Printed by *The Oregonian.* Feb. 25, 1886.

Chan, Sucheng; Wong, K. Scott. Claiming America: Constructing Chinese American Identities during the Exclusion Era. Temple University Press, Philadelphia. 1998.

Cheung, David. Christianity in Modern China: The Making of

the First Native Protestant Church. Brill, Boston. 2004.

City of San Francisco. "The Virtual Museum of the City of San Francisco." Accessed various times in 2013

Daniels, Roger. Asian America: Chinese and Japanese in the United States since 1850. University of Washington Press, 1988.

Edholm, M.G.C. "A Stain on the Flag." *Californian Illustrated Magazine*, Vol. 1. 1892.

Foner, Philip S. and Rosenberg, Daniel. Racism, Dissent, and Asian Americans from 1850 to the Present: A Documentary History. Greenwood Press, Westport, CT. 1993.

Gardner, Martha. The Qualities of a Citizen: Women, Immigration, and Citizenship, 1870-1965. Princeton University Press, Princeton, NJ. 2005.

Genthe, Arnold. *As I Remember.* Reynal & Hitchcock, New York. 1936.

Gibson, Eliza. "A Trip to China." *California Christian Advocate* of 1916.

Grey, Helen. "Confession of a Chinese Slave-Dealer." *The Call,* San Francisco. April 2, 1899. Accessed July 3, 2013.

Grossi, Patricia. Muir-Wood, Robert. *The 1906 San Francisco Earthquake and Fire: Perspectives on a Modern Super Cat.* Risk Management Solutions, Newark, NJ. 2006.

Hardy, Gayle J. American Women Civil Rights Activists: Bio-bibliographies of 68 Leaders, 1825-1992. McFarland, Jefferson, NC. 1993.

Harvard University. *California Gold Rush (1848–1858)*. Accessed 6/19/13.

Hum Lee, Rose. *The Chinese in the United States of America.* Hong Kong University Press, Hong Kong. 1960.

Irwin, Will. The City That Was: A Requiem of Old San Francisco. Project Gutenberg. 2009.

Jane Troutman. "'06 quake through eyes of woman ahead of her time." *San Francisco Gate (San Francisco Chronicle),* April 16, 2011.

Jorae, Wendy Rouse. The Children of Chinatown: Growing Up Chinese American in San Francisco, 1850-1920. University of North Carolina Press, Chapel Hill, NC. 2009.

Kalloch, Isaac Smith. "Chinatown Declared a Nuisance!" Pamphlet published by the Workingmen's Committee of California, San Francisco. 1880.

Kim, Hyung-Chan. *Dictionary of Asian American History.* Greenwood Press, New York. 1986.

Lee, Anthony W. *Picturing Chinatown: Art and Orientalism in San Francisco.* University of California Press, Berkeley, CA. 2001.

Lee, Erika. At America's Gates: Chinese Immigration during the Exclusion Era, 1882-1943. University of North Carolina Press, Chapel Hill, NC. 2003.

Library of Congress. The Chinese in California, 1850-1925.

Ling, Huping. Surviving on the Gold Mountain: A History of Chinese American Women and Their Lives. University of New York Pres, Albany, NY. 1998.

Luibhéid, Eithne. *Entry Denied: Controlling Sexuality at the Border.* University of Minnesota Press, Minneapolis. 2002.

Milner II, Clyde A. A New Significance: Re-Envisioning the History of the American West. Oxford University Press, New York. 1996.

Norton, Henry K. The Story of California from the Earliest Days to the Present. A.C. McClurg & Co., Chicago. 1924.

Pascoe, Peggy. Relations of Rescue: The Search for Female Moral Authority in the American West, 1874-1939. Oxford US, New York. 1993

The Gold Rush: An American Experience. www.pbs.org.

Perkins, William. El Campo de los Sonoraenses or: Three years residence in California.

Public Opinion: Comprehensive Summary of The Press throughout the World on all Important Current Topics. Volume XXXVII. Public Opinion, New York. 1904.

Pyke, J.H. "Missionary Preaching: What It Is and How It Is Done." *World-Wide Evangelization: the Urgent Business of the Church.* New York, 1902.

Quaife, Milo Milton. *Pictures of Gold Rush California.* Lakeside Press, Chicago. 1949.

Read, Phil. "Ah Toy -- Woman of the West." The Museum of Art and History at the McPherson Center, Santa Cruz, CA.

Report of the Chinese Mission to the California Conference of the Methodist Episcopal Church 1893. Cubby and Company, San Francisco. 1893.

Robbins, Pauline F. "Our Forty Years." *New Era Magazine,* Volume 26, Issues 1-7. Published by the Presbyterian Church.

"Chinese transformed 'Gold Mountain'". *Sacramento Bee.*

Seventy-Fourth Annual Report of the Missionary Society of the Methodist Episcopal Church for the Year 1892. MEC, New York. 1892.

Staley, Jeffrey L.

Staley, Jeffrey L. "Gum Moon": The First Fifty Years of Methodist Women's Work in San Francisco Chinatown, 1870-1920." *The Argonaut* (Journal of the San Francisco Museum and Historical Society), Vol. 16:1. 2005.

Ling, Huping. Surviving on the Gold Mountain: A History of

Chinese American Women and Their Lives. State University of New York Press, Albany, NY. 1998.

The Church at Home and Abroad, Volume 22. Edited by Henry Addison Nelson, Albert B. Robinson. Presbyterian Church in the U.S.A. 1899.

Norton, Henry K. The Story of California from the Earliest Days to the Present. A.C. McClurg & Co., Chicago. 1924.

The Western Christian Advocate, Volume 69

Tomkinson, Laura E. *Twenty years' history of the Woman's home missionary society of the Methodist Episcopal Church 1880-1900.* The Woman's home missionary society of the Methodist Episcopal Church. Cincinnati. 1903.

White, Katherine A. A Yankee Trader in the Gold Rush: The Letters of Franklin A. Buck. Houghton Mifflin Co., Boston. 1930.

Women's Foreign Missionary of the Presbyterian Church. *Woman's Work Vol. 27.* Presbyterian Church of the U.S.A., New York. 1912.

World-wide Evangelization the Urgent Business of the Church. Student Volunteer Movement for Foreign Missions. International Convention, Ontario, 1902.

Wyatt, David. Five Fires: Race, Catastrophe, and the Shaping of California. Addison-Wesley, Reading, MA. 1997.

Yung, Judy. Unbound Voices: A Documentary History of Chinese Women in San Francisco. University of California Press. 1999.

Yung, Judy; Chang, Gordon; Lai, Mark. *Chinese American Voices: From the Gold Rush to the Present.* University of California Press, 2006.

The Devil Came Down to Chinatown

About the Author

Dr. Christine Taylor, D.Min. (Dr. Chris) is a speaker, teacher, writer, actress, and storyteller. Her mission is to help Christian woman launch their own glorious adventures with God.

Visit www.doctorchris.org to find more her blog, books, articles, and retreats.

Other Books by Dr. Chris

The Living Story: Learning to Pray the Gospels

14411677R10151

Made in the USA
Lexington, KY
07 November 2018